9/05

Terrorist
Leaders

Other books in the
Profiles in History series:

Black Abolitionists
Black Women Activists
Leaders of the Civil Rights Movement

Terrorist Leaders

Profiles · in · History

Mitchell Young, *Book Editor*

Bruce Glassman, *Vice President*
Bonnie Szumski, *Publisher*
Helen Cothran, *Managing Editor*

GREENHAVEN PRESS
An imprint of Thomson Gale, a part of The Thomson Corporation

THOMSON
——————
GALE

Detroit • New York • San Francisco • San Diego • New Haven, Conn.
Waterville, Maine • London • Munich

LIBRARY OF CONGRESS CATALOGING-IN-PUBLICATION DATA

Terrorist leaders / Mitchell Young, book editor.
    p. cm. — (Profiles in history)
Includes bibliographical references and index.
ISBN 0-7377-2649-0 (lib. : alk. paper)
    1. Terrorism. 2. National liberation movements. I. Young, Mitchell. II. Series.
HV6431. T535 2005
303.6'25'0922—dc22   2004047446

Printed in the United States of America

Contents

Chapter 1: Osama bin Laden and al Qaeda

1. Bin Laden's Efforts in the Afghan War

by Yossef Bodansky   25

While fighting Soviet troops in Afghanistan during the 1980s, Osama bin Laden gained knowledge and experience he would later put to use in
his terrorist campaign against the West.

2. Bin Laden Establishes a Pan-Islamic Terrorist Network

by John L. Esposito   33

Following the Soviet withdrawal from Afghanistan, Bin Laden returned to the Middle East to
finance and build a loosely organized network of
militant Islamicists and supporters, his enemy
now the democratic West.

3. Bin Laden Speaks About His Plans for an Islamic Revolution

by Peter L. Bergen   45

In a rare 1997 interview, Osama bin Laden
spelled out his complaints against the West and
the United States and issued an ominous
warning.

Chapter 2: Dictators and State Terror

effort to eliminate both modern and traditional cultural influences, millions perished.

Chapter 3: Terrorism and National Liberation

Chapter 4: Ideological Terrorists

Foreword

Historians and other scholars have often argued about which forces are most influential in driving the engines of history. A favorite theory in past ages was that powerful supernatural forces—the gods and/or fate—were deciding factors in earthly events. Modern theories, by contrast, have tended to emphasize more natural and less mysterious factors. In the nineteenth century, for example, the great Scottish historian Thomas Carlyle stated, "No great man lives in vain. The history of the world is but the biography of great men." This was the kernel of what came to be known as the "great man" theory of history, the idea that from time to time an unusually gifted, influential man or woman emerges and pushes the course of civilization in a new direction. According to Carlyle:

> Universal History, the history of what man has accomplished in this world, is at bottom the History of the Great Men who have worked here. They were the leaders of men, these great ones; the modelers . . . of whatsoever the general mass of men contrived to do or to attain; all things that we see standing accomplished in the world are properly the outer material result. . . . The soul of the whole world's history, it may justly be considered, were the history of these [persons].

In this view, individuals such as Moses, Buddha, Augustus, Christ, Constantine, Elizabeth I, Thomas Jefferson, Frederick Douglass, Franklin Roosevelt, and Nelson

Mandela accomplished deeds or promoted ideas that sooner or later reshaped human societies in large portions of the globe.

The great man thesis, which was widely popular in the late 1800s and early 1900s, has since been eclipsed by other theories of history. Some scholars accept the "situational" theory. It holds that human leaders and innovators only react to social situations and movements that develop substantially on their own, through random interactions. In this view, Moses achieved fame less because of his unique personal qualities and more because he wisely dealt with the already existing situation of the Hebrews wandering in the desert in search of a new home.

More widely held, however, is a view that in a sense combines the great man and situational theories. Here, major historical periods and political, social, and cultural movements occur when a group of gifted, influential, and like-minded individuals respond to a situation or need over the course of time. In this scenario, Moses is seen as one of a group of prophets who over the course of centuries established important traditions of monotheism; and over time a handful of ambitious, talented pharaohs led ancient Egypt from its emergence as the world's first nation to its great age of conquest and empire. Likewise, the Greek playwrights Sophocles and Euripides, the Elizabethan playwright Shakespeare, and the American playwright Eugene O'Neill all advanced the art of drama, leading it to its present form.

The books in the Profiles in History series chronicle and examine in detail the leading figures in some of history's most important historical periods and movements. Some, like those covering Egypt's leading pharaohs and the most influential U.S. presidents, deal with national leaders guiding a great people through good times and bad. Other volumes in the series examine the leaders of important, constructive social movements, such as those that sought to abolish slavery in the nineteenth century and fought for human rights in the twentieth century. And some, such as the one on Hitler and his henchmen, profile far less constructive, though no less historically important, groups of leaders.

Each book in the series begins with a detailed essay providing crucial background information on the historical period or movement being covered. The main body of the volume consists of a series of shorter essays, each covering an important individual in that period or movement. Where appropriate, two or more essays are devoted to a particularly influential person. Some of the essays provide biographical information; while others, including primary sources by or about the person, focus in on his or her specific deeds, ideas, speeches, or followers. More primary source documents, providing further detail, appear in an appendix, followed by a chronology of events and a thorough, up-to-date bibliography that guides interested readers to further research. Overall, the volumes of the Profiles in History series offer a balanced view of the march of civilization by demonstrating how certain individuals make history and at the same time are products of the deeds and movements of their predecessors.

Introduction

Terrorism is a political strategy that depends on violence, or the threat of violence, to intimidate a government or civilian population to achieve a political goal. Its modern adherents follow a long historical precedent. Indeed, the organized, intentional use of terror for political ends goes back at least to the late eighteenth century, when radical French revolutionaries instigated the Reign of Terror to remake their country's society. Terror has been a tactic of anarchists, workers, and governments throughout the nineteenth and twentieth centuries; it is a major international threat at the beginning of the twenty-first century.

Of course, radical social change can be achieved without terrorist tactics. In democratic societies voting in elections can bring about change. Mass protest or civil disobedience has been successful in transforming some undemocratic societies. Even revolution, which can be violent, is different from terrorism in that terrorism seeks to overturn the status quo by inducing fear through murder and destruction among innocent people.

Terrorists' Motivations and Strategies

Typically, groups that turn to terrorism are too small to engage the forces of the government they want to change directly. They are too weak to attack military targets or even police. Instead they turn to attacking civilian targets in the hope that they can intimidate or coerce society into granting their demands. On the other hand, some of the worst terror in history has been carried out by governments who wish to terrorize their own citizens into behaving as the government thinks they should. The common factor is inducing fear.

Because the goal is to create fear in a general populace, terror is random. It is not usually directed against military targets or specific individuals. Instead whole populations become targets. Individuals, regardless of guilt or innocence, military or civilian status, government official or private citizen become targets for the terrorist. The justification for this random violence is a fanatic belief that the terrorist act serves a just and necessary cause, righting some fundamental wrong or achieving the highest good.

Aside from this common goal, however, terrorists are motivated by a range of causes that experts group into four main categories.

Terrorism in the Name of Religion

Every terrorist is a true believer. He believes in the justice of his cause. The religious terrorist believes he or she is practicing the true faith; by bombing a train or flying an airplane into a building he or she is carrying out the will of God. Only the violence of such acts can bring about the redemption of a wicked world or the destruction of the enemies of God. The terrorist becomes an instrument of the wrath of God. Often he or she believes that God will reward the terrorist in the afterlife for successfully carrying out the act of terror, especially if the act involves personal martyrdom.

This is the motivation of terrorist leader Osama bin Laden and his followers in the Islamic terrorist organization al Qaeda. They see the world as divided between those who refuse to follow the true path of Islam and true believers who are being assaulted by the forces of evil and who need defenders. To Bin Laden and the young men of al Qaeda, the forces of evil have been represented by two "infidel" superpowers.

The Soviet Union was Bin Laden's first opponent. In 1979 the Communist superpower invaded Afghanistan to support the Communist government of that country. Islamic fighters who objected to the Communists' program of modernization and secularization of the country, called mujahideen, were trying to overthrow the government. Seeing fellow Muslims pitted against the much stronger Soviet army, Bin Laden went to neighboring Pakistan to offer his assistance to the Islamic mujahideen.

The Afghan conflict was truly of worldwide significance. Many of the Soviet officers were true believers in communism; they fought with the ruthlessness borne of that belief. The Russians attacked villages with helicopter gunships and are charged with using poison gas on the Afghan civilian population. On the other side of the conflict were the mujahideen. These young men were volunteers from all over the Islamic world. At first they fought with little in the way of weapons or organization. As the world took notice of their struggle, however, they began to gather support. The United States funded them and supplied weapons in an attempt to hurt its superpower rival, the Soviet Union. With time, more volunteers made their way to Afghanistan to carry the fight to the "infidel" Communists.

It was this jihad in Afghanistan, which after ten years of struggle achieved its aim of driving out the Soviets, that prompted the growth of an international network of radical Islamicists. This network eventually became known as al Qaeda. It consists of spiritual leaders who interpret the "will of God" for a cadre of young terrorists who carry out acts designed to further the cause of Islam.

Unfortunately for the Western world, after the defeat of the Soviets, these terrorists soon turned their sights to the other superpower, the United States. The United States was seen as the new great enemy. The Gulf War of 1991 strengthened this belief. In that conflict to oust Iraq from Kuwait, the United States was directly fighting against Muslims for the first time. It also involved the stationing of large numbers of American troops in the Middle East. For Bin Laden, a native Saudi, the presence of these infidel troops in Arab lands, and especially in Saudi Arabia, meant this holy area was defiled.

Another point of conflict for Islamicists was the continuing support of the United States for the Jewish state of Israel, the sworn enemy of many Arab states since 1948. Israel represented a permanent non-Muslim presence in the Middle East, and its creation had displaced large Palestinian populations and led to Israeli occupation of the West Bank, formerly under Arab control. Islamicists of al Qaeda believed that the United States and the West in general cared little about the plight of these Muslims.

These complaints caused many of the same mujahideen who had benefited from U.S. support in Afghanistan to turn against their benefactor. America was the new target of the jihad. Al Qaeda carried out a series of terrorist attacks against the United States in the 1990s. The first major incident was the bombing of the World Trade Center in New York in 1993. This incident was followed by attacks against U.S. military barracks in Saudi Arabia and the American embassy in Nairobi, Kenya. The attacks culminated in the September 11 attacks on the World Trade Center and Pentagon in 2001. In interviews after the 9/11 attacks, Osama bin Laden praised the piety of the Muslim suicide squads who carried out these deeds and asked Allah to let them enter paradise. The U.S.-led coalition in Iraq in 2003 has provoked threats of similar international attacks and continuing terrorist incidents in the Middle East targeting civilians, U.S. troops, and Muslims accused of collaborating with the West.

State Terror

Today terrorism is most closely associated with violence conducted by small groups of religious militants, but the term *terror* was first used to describe the campaign of extreme violence conducted by the state after the French Revolution. The "great terror," which began in 1792 and ended in 1794, was a means of purging French society of intellectual and aristocratic elites that had been in power in prerevolutionary society. In this way the revolutionary leaders on the so-called Committee of Public Safety—Maximilien Robespierre, Louis Antoine Léon de Saint-Just, and others—hoped to effect a complete break with the past.

In the twentieth century other dictators emulated the great terror tactics of Robespierre. In the 1930s the Soviet Union experienced Joseph Stalin's great purges and police state. Mao Zedong instituted the terror of the Cultural Revolution in 1960s China. The last great terror of the twentieth century was Pol Pot's brutal regime in Cambodia, during which one-third of Cambodia's population perished in the so-called killing fields. All of these leaders attempted a radical remaking of the existing society by bending a fearful, oppressed people to the leader's ideological will.

State terror is in some ways a reverse of terrorism by a powerless or disenfranchised radical minority. In these cases it is a powerful government imposing its will on the people. Sometimes the terror is directed against those said to have carried out "counterrevolutionary" or other crimes against the revolutionary state.

Its terrorist nature may be disguised by formal charges and show trials. However, it is terrorism in that any member of society can become a victim, no matter how supportive of the revolution. A veneer of formal legal proceedings actually does nothing to shield innocent individuals from harm. In the Soviet purges of the 1930s, for example, many devoted revolutionaries were put on trial and eventually executed—not for opposing the Soviet state per se, but for opposing Stalin's methods or ideology. Guilty verdicts, even the accusations themselves, had little to do with the accused's actual activities.

The leaders of state terror in the twentieth century tried to institute a radical political program. Stalin sought to transform the Soviet Union from an agricultural economy to an industrial power. To achieve this he forced peasants to give up their own land and join giant collective farms. The resulting disruption of food supplies caused massive famine—exacerbated when Stalin withheld food from some regions in order to force the peasants to go along with his collectivization program. Stalin's network of secret police and informants cultivated a climate of fear in which anyone seen as insufficiently committed to Stalin could be charged with crimes against the Soviet state. Such accusations were so widespread and without foundation as to be almost random. Anyone, no matter how loyal to the Communist Party, could be charged with crimes against the state.

Like Stalin, the Cambodian dictator Pol Pot tried to radically transform his country's society. But where Stalin sought modernization and industrialization, Pol Pot wanted the opposite. After coming to power in 1975, he devised a plan to return Cambodia to a supposed golden age in which the country was completely agricultural and free of foreign influence. To that end his repression targeted the urban population of Cambodia. Educated, wealthy people were killed; entire cities were emptied by youth armies who herded people into forced resettlements in the countryside. Hundreds of thousands died of harsh treatment; lack of food, water, housing, or sanitation; and brutal punishment based on advanced education, knowledge of a foreign language, or some other connection to foreigners. The Cambodian killing fields only ended when the Vietnamese invaded the country and overthrew the dictator in 1979.

The above examples show how dictators can use the power of the state to sow terror in the populace. Indeed, these state terrorists have historically been the most deadly criminals. However, the fact that they were in a position of ruler of a sovereign state has made charges of terrorism difficult to prosecute. Some such as Pol Pot were eventually charged with crimes when overthrown. Yet many state terrorists have gone to peaceful deaths, never having to face justice for their crimes.

Terror for National Liberation

A third category of terrorist includes those motivated by the desire to free their nation from foreign control. Rather than controlling the armed forces of the state, they fight against those forces. Nationalist movements are too weak, however, to directly engage powerful occupation or foreign authorities, so terrorists seek political destabilization by attacking civilian targets, whether property or population. More than other categories, in terrorism for national liberation the line between freedom fighter and terrorist is blurred, and terrorism is harder to define.

An example is the Algerian national liberation front of Ahmed Ben Bella. In the late 1950s and early 1960s this movement sought to free Algeria from French colonial rule. Ben Bella also fought the dominance of French settlers, many of whom had lived in the country for generations and controlled a large part of the best farming land. Known as the FLN, the movement was weak compared with the French armed forces. In addition, it had to battle militias set up by French settlers. To counteract their disadvantage Ben Bella chose to attack civilian targets. Some attacks were against state institutions such as post offices. Others were carried out against sites where Europeans were known to congregate, such as cafés in the European quarters of Algerian cities. At times specific people were targeted, such as Algerian Arabs, who were suspected of collaborating with the French. The result of these attacks was an escalation of terror, with the settlers' militia engaging in reprisals against Algerian Arab civilians. Ultimately, however, the FLN's strategy was successful; France gave up control of Algeria.

The case of Israel versus Palestine shows the sometimes ambiguous nature of terrorism carried out in the name of national liberation. In late 1940s Palestine, Jewish settlers used terror tactics against both the British (who ruled the area by mandate) and Palestinian Arab civilians. The British were targeted because they were an obstacle to the establishment of a Jewish state in the region. The Arabs were targeted to make them flee and reduce the threat of Arab attack, thus creating a state that had an overwhelming Jewish majority. Some of the leaders of these terrorist acts, such as Menachem Begin and Yitzhak Rabin, went on to lead Israel. They were opposed by Palestinian leader Yasir Arafat, who used terror against Israel in order to win a state for the displaced Palestinians. Especially in the case of terror for national liberation, one man's terrorist can be another's freedom fighter.

Terror in the Service of Ideology

National liberation movements seek to change who rules a society. Their goal is to remove foreign control and replace it with native control. Sometimes this change is to be accompanied by a radical change in economy or some other aspect of society, but this is not critical. In contrast, ideological terrorist movements seek not only to change who is in control, but also seek deep and radical change throughout a society based on an often personal vision. Their motivation ranges from political to economic to cultural, and ideological terrorists are less likely to attract a wide following. Indeed, in some cases they are "movements" of a single individual with grievances and the means to act violently.

The Baader-Meinhof gang of Germany is a typical example of a small ideological terrorist group. It never had more than a few dozen members, yet was able to attack several significant targets in 1970s West Germany. These young adults were motivated by what they saw as a corrupt capitalist society in West Germany. This view was supplemented by guilt over their parents' generation's deeds during World War II. As Baader-Meinhof saw it, German society was so corrupt it needed to be destroyed and completely rebuilt on some sort of Marxist program. The gang carried out a spree of bombings, shootings, and robberies in the early 1970s to publicize their radical agenda and press for political change. The hope was to spark a revolution of "the workers," but they ended up being held in contempt by the German populace.

American terrorist Timothy McVeigh and some members of the U.S. militia movement were similar to Baader-Meinhof in their desire to completely remake the structure of society. Where Baader-Meinhof wanted to spark revolution among German workers, McVeigh hoped to provoke a rebellion against the U.S. federal government. Yet McVeigh and the movement he represented were most emphatically not Marxist. They sought to drastically limit the power of government, especially the federal government. When the government attacked a religious cult's compound in Waco, Texas, in April 1993, the militia movement saw this as an act of war on liberty. McVeigh thus felt justified in carrying out his bombing of the federal building in Oklahoma City in April 1995. He was, he believed, legitimately responding to the government's declaration of war against its own people. McVeigh hoped that his actions would ignite a general revolt against the government and lead to the breakup of the United States.

Theodore Kaczynski—the so-called Unabomber—was not at war with the government of the United States; he was at war with the industrial economy. He blamed the industrial system for destroying the pristine wilderness he loved so much. Timothy McVeigh targeted a federal government building; Kaczynski sent bombs to leaders of industry and scientific researchers. These were the people he saw as making industrial society possible. His attacks in the 1980s and 1990s finally came to an end when his brother recognized his "Manifesto," published by several newspapers as an attempt to appease the Unabomber.

Both McVeigh and Kaczynski attacked targets that their ideologies identified as the enemy. However, their worldview was not accepted by the vast majority of the people in America.

Conclusion: More of the Same?

As the above examples show, there are many different sorts of terrorist leaders and terrorist groups. Some, like Stalin and Mao, operate at the very center of power, using the might of the state to terrorize the societies over which they rule. Contrasting with these state dictators are marginalized figures, such as Theodore Kaczynski and Timothy McVeigh, who are not well integrated into society and who operate alone or with a few coconspirators. In between these extremes are terrorists of national liberation and terrorists who operate in groups. Yet all these terrorists have one thing in common; they all want quick and radical change in society.

Terror will no doubt continue into the future because the sad truth is that it often works. People *do* live in fear of speaking out. People *do* accommodate a brutal order when the threat of violence is clear. Individuals who are deeply dissatisfied with present social structures will be willing to commit acts of violence to change these structures. Some will be recruited by existing networks of terrorists, such as al Qaeda. Other disaffected young men and women will form new groups that choose violence to achieve their objectives. With society's ever-increasing ease of global communication and movement, people devoted to a cause will find ways to communicate and organize.

Experts predict a mix of differing types of terror. Of course there has always been some overlap, as evidenced by Carlos the Jackal, a terrorist who served both Marxist ideology and causes of national liberation. A newer mix features not Marxism, but Islam combined with national liberation. For example, on the West Bank of the Jordan River, Palestinians are using terror to carry out a national liberation struggle against Israeli occupiers. This conflict has been going on since the late 1960s, but militant Islam has been increasingly influential in what was previously a secular national liberation movement. In practice this means that seemingly desperate acts such as suicide bombing are replacing the careful tactics of the secular Palestinian guerrillas. Such tactics are also being used against American troops and their allies in Iraq. Unfortunately, a religiously motivated terrorist willing to sacrifice his or her own life in carrying out a bombing or murder is more difficult to stop than a terrorist who wishes to escape with his or her life. This mixing of Islam and national liberation will likely prove to be the most dangerous form of terror in the next decades.

On the other hand, the era of state terror seems to be over for the time being. Russia is now on the way to democracy, and the Chinese government has found it is more productive to maintain a political dictatorship while leaving many elements of society, such as the economy, functioning freely. Ironically, the exception to this easing of state terror comes when movements of national or religious liberation erupt. The Chinese have used terror tactics to quell nationalist rebellion in Tibet and to stop the Falun Gong religious movement.

While the future of terrorism cannot be predicted with certainty, study of past patterns may allow some insight into how, when, where, and why terrorists of the future will operate. It is especially important to understand terrorist leaders, as these individuals will ultimately make the decisions on when and where terrorists strike. The following articles profile of some of the most dangerous and effective terrorist leaders, of all categories. All share the desire to provoke swift and radical change in society. The articles that follow will lead the reader to make his or her own conclusions about the motivations of past terrorist leaders and the sorts of terrorist movements that might arise in the future.

Profiles · in · History

Osama bin Laden
and al Qaeda

Bin Laden's Efforts in the Afghan War

Yossef Bodansky

In 1979 the Soviet Union invaded the predominantly Muslim country of Afghanistan. The invasion prompted many young men from throughout the Muslim world to go to Afghanistan and fight. Among them was Osama bin Laden.

Born in 1957, Bin Laden had led a comfortable existence as the son of a wealthy Saudi construction contractor. The fighting in Afghanistan changed his life. It was in Afghanistan that Bin Laden gained practical experience in organizing Muslims to fight a jihad, or holy war. Here Bin Laden found his life's calling as a holy warrior who would go on to orchestrate numerous terrorist attacks.

In addition to authoring several books on terrorism, Yossef Bodansky has served as the director of the U.S. Congressional Task Force on Terrorism and Unconventional Warfare. In the following excerpt, he explains how Bin Laden used the organizational skills learned in the construction business to build an international terrorist network.

🐾 🐾 🐾

Osama bin Laden was one of the first Arabs to go to Afghanistan after the Soviet invasion. "I was enraged and went there at once," he said to an Arab journalist. In retrospect, bin Laden now considers the Soviet invasion of Afghanistan a turning point in his life. "The Soviet Union invaded Afghanistan, and the mujahideen [Islamic 'Holy Warriors'] put out an international plea for help," he explained to another interviewer. He was inspired by the plight of Muslims "in a medieval society besieged by a twentieth-century superpower. . . . In our religion, there is a special place in the hereafter for those who participate in jihad [Holy War]," he added. "One day in Afghanistan was like one thousand days of praying in an ordinary mosque."

Within a few days after the Soviet invasion bin Laden, who was genuinely and selflessly committed to the cause of all-Islamic solidarity, went to Pakistan to assist the Afghan mujahideen. On arrival bin Laden was appalled by the chaos in Pakistan and the lack of Arab unity and devoted himself to political and organizational work, establishing a recruitment drive that over the next few years would funnel thousands of Arab fighters from the Gulf States to the Afghan resistance. At first he personally covered the travel costs of these volunteers to Pakistan and Afghanistan, but more important, he set up the main camps to train them. In early 1980 bin Laden established Ma'sadat Al-Ansar, then the main base for Arab mujahideen in Afghanistan. . . .

Bin Laden's Know-How Helps the Terrorist Cause

Bin Laden had money, knowledge, and enthusiasm and implemented Azzam's [Sheikh AbdAllah Yussuf Azzam, an ideologist of militant Islam] ideas. Azzam and bin Laden established the Maktab al-Khidamat—the Mujahideen Services Bureau—which bin Laden soon transformed into an international network that sought out Islamists with special knowledge, from medical doctors and engineers to terrorists and drug smugglers, and re-cruited them for service in Afghanistan. By the late 1980s bin Laden would have branches and recruitment centers in fifty countries, including the United States, Egypt, Saudi Arabia, and some Western European countries. While handling the arrival and deployment of numerous Arabs, bin Laden noticed that they needed training and conditioning before they confronted the harsh conditions in Afghanistan. So Azzam and bin Laden next established Masadat Al-Ansar—the central base and home-away-from-home for the Arab mu-jahideen in both Afghanistan and Pakistan. In the course of these activities bin Laden made contacts with numer-ous Islamist leaders and mujahideen from every corner of the world—relations that now prove invaluable in his jihad against the United States.

Building Fortifications for the Afghan Jihad

Appalled by the mujahideen's vulnerability to Soviet and DRA [Democratic Republic of Afghanistan] ar-tillery, bin Laden brought heavy engineering equip-ment from Saudi Arabia. He first rushed some of the family's bulldozers to Afghanistan to expedite the con-struction of roads and facilities for the mujahideen in eastern Afghanistan. Soon afterward he organized the delivery of diversified heavy equipment from numerous Saudi and other Gulf Arab companies, using the equip-ment to dig trenches and shelters for the mujahideen. The Soviets, fully aware of the importance of these for-tifications, launched numerous helicopter gunship strikes against bin Laden's bulldozers. Many times he continued working under fire, oblivious to the danger. With military help pouring in, bin Laden trained Afghans, Pakistanis, and fellow Arabs to use the heavy engineering equipment. He then embarked on an am-bitious program to build a fortified infrastructure for the mujahideen in eastern Afghanistan, building with his crews roads, tunnels, hospitals, and storage depots.

By 1980 the United States was pressuring Arab governments to take a more active role in the Afghanistan crisis. [Egyptian] President [Anwar] Sadat agreed to help the fledgling Afghan resistance with weapons. Publicly Sadat claimed to provide Egyptian military assistance "because they are our Muslim brothers and in trouble." This enabled the Islamists to agitate the population in the name of Afghanistan and also to find a safe haven outside Egypt for some of their people, especially those linked to the assassination of Sadat in October 1981. Egyptian journalist and commentator Mohamed Heikal observed that since "Afghanistan was to be helped in the name of Islamic solidarity, that was playing into the hands of the unofficial Muslim groups, which were in a much better position to exploit it." Indeed, in early 1980 a few Egyptian Islamists, some of them former officers in the Egyptian army, began arriving in Afghanistan to share their military knowledge with the mujahideen. Many of the first Egyptians to arrive were led by Ahmad Shawqi al-Islambuli, currently [in 2001] one of bin Laden's senior terrorist commanders and the brother of Khalid al-Islambuli, Sadat's assassin. They were fugitives from purges in Egypt, and they soon established a cohesive Arab revolutionary and terrorist movement that still constitutes the hard core of bin Laden's key commanders and most trusted troops. Meanwhile, in 1983 Islambuli organized a network in Karachi for smuggling people and weapons to and from Egypt that is still functioning. But ultimately, from 1980 to 1982, the Arab world was mute on the issue of Afghanistan.

In the early 1980s Osama bin Laden returned home to organize financial support for the mujahideen and for the recruitment and transport of volunteers. Toward

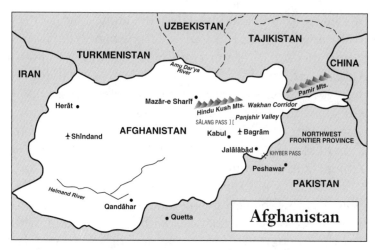

this end he utilized the contacts his family had with the uppermost echelons in Riyadh. He soon established contacts with Prince Salman, the king's brother; Prince Turki; the chief of intelligence; and other key officials.

Although bin Laden was urging all-out support for the Afghan jihad, Riyadh had other priorities and plans for the well-connected young militant. At the time the idea of a strategic encirclement and pincer movement by pro-Soviet forces in the Arabian Peninsula terrified the Saudis. They were most alarmed by the growing Soviet, East German, and Cuban military presence in South Yemen—then officially a Communist state, the PDRY [Peoples Democratic Republic of Yemen]—and the Horn of Africa just across the Red Sea. While Saudi Arabia was officially conducting a policy of appeasement and economic inducement toward the PDRY, Riyadh had other ideas in mind.

Saudi intelligence sponsored a clandestine Islamist insurgency in the PDRY, ostensibly under the banner of Tariq al-Fadli, the last sultan of Aden and a militant Islamist. Osama bin Laden was asked to form "volunteer" mujahideen units to bolster the ranks of the Adeni anti-Communist insurgents. This endeavor was fully funded by Riyadh and blessed by the highest authorities in the Saudi Court. Bin Laden established strike forces from a mixture of Islamist volunteers planning to go to Afghanistan and Saudi White Guards special forces that were seconded (formally put on leave). Bin Laden was so involved in the PDRY struggle that he even participated in several raids and clashes with the South Yemeni security forces. But despite the enthusiasm the Yemeni anti-Communist jihad never really took off. With no tangible success in sight, Riyadh pulled the plug. By now, however, bin Laden had already established close personal relations with Tariq al-Fadli, who was then deported to Sana; he and other Yemeni Islamist commanders bin Laden met and helped in the early 1980s would help him in the 1990s.

Osama bin Laden's enthusiasm, commitment, and efficiency in running the Yemeni endeavor were not lost on the Saudi Court. After the conclusion of the special operations against the PDRY, Riyadh sought to consummate the special relations with the young bin Laden through binding and most lucrative financial arrangements. In the early 1980s the Saudi Court decided to expand the two holy mosques. The project would have gone to one of [Osama's father] Muhammad bin Laden's companies, but to honor Osama, King Fahd personally offered him the contract for expanding the Prophet's Mosque in Medina. He was told that this deal alone would net him a profit of $90 million. In an audience with King Fahd, Osama bin Laden refused the offer and instead argued passionately for greater commitment to and support for the jihad in Afghanistan. King Fahd, Crown Prince Abdallah, and Prince Turki, already convinced of the strategic importance of the situation in Afghanistan for Saudi Arabia, were strongly influenced by bin Laden's conviction and promised to help the Afghan "cause." In the end Osama did not lose much financially, for the contract went to his father. Osama later told confidants in Afghanistan that his wealth increased and his business grew with the amount of money he spent on the jihad.

The Mujahideen Movement Gathers Strength

Despite the efforts of the Afghan mujahideen, the impact of Afghanistan on the Muslim world grew only in the mid-1980s, when media exposure increased and organized transportation, originated by Osama bin Laden, was institutionalized. Until then even the Arab Islamists, preoccupied with the struggle against their own governments, seemed indifferent. But in 1985 hundreds of Arabs, predominantly Islamists, began joining the ranks of the Afghan mujahideen. In the early 1980s some 3,000 to 3,500 Arabs were in Afghanistan; by the mid-1980s there were some 16,000 to 20,000 associated with Hizb-i Islami (Party of Islam) alone. Arab Islamist organizations also sent some of their commanders to Afghanistan to study the jihad. In the mujahideen camps they received the kind of advanced Islamic education forbidden in many Arab states as subversive or seditious.

These foreign volunteers were easily absorbed into the Muslim environment in Pakistan because of the all-Islamic ideological character of the Afghan resistance. In the mid-1980s the Iranian analyst Amir Taheri elucidated the nature of the resistance: "The Afghan resistance movement has not confined itself to a minimum program of securing the nation's independence and territorial integrity, but openly advocates the creation of an Islamic society. It is in the name of Allah, and not of nationalism in the Western meaning of the term, that Soviet troops are gunned down in the mountains of Afghanistan. In some of the liberated zones the resistance movement has already brought into existence its ideal Islamic society. Here, women have been pushed back into the veil, polygamy has been legalized, girls are kept out of school, and the mullahs and mawlavis [religious leaders] exercise their tyrannical power in all spheres of life." All of these social values and objectives were identical to the aspirations of the arriving Arabs, especially those from the Muslim Brotherhood—the original and still the most religiously authoritative Sunni Islamist organization—and the various jihadist organizations.

Afghanistan Is a Training Ground

By the mid-1980s Afghanistan had become a magnet for militant Islamists from all over the world. In the early 1980s it hadn't taken long for Egyptian and other Arab Islamist groups to begin using Peshawar as a center for their headquarters in exile. As a result of their growing cooperation, they established an "international jihad organization" using Pakistan and Afghanistan as their springboard for operations back home. For example, one of the first jihad movement bureaus was opened in 1984 by Dr. Ayman al-Zawahiri for the Islamic jihad movement of Abbud al-Zumur, a lieutenant-colonel in Egyptian military intelligence and a senior clandestine military commander of the Islamic jihad who was arrested on the eve of Sadat's assassination. Zawahiri escaped from Egypt in the mid-1980s, during the anti-Islamist purges launched by President [Hosni] Mubarak, who took over after Sadat was killed. Zawahiri is presently bin Laden's closest companion and the senior military commander of his "movement." Members of this first generation of foreign volunteers in Afghanistan, all of whom are fiercely loyal to bin Laden, now constitute the leadership and high command of the Islamist terrorist movement. The Egyptian contingent of the international mujahideen would reach singular importance in the early 1990s as a leading element of the terrorist surge into the West.

Bin Laden Establishes a Pan-Islamic Terrorist Network

John L. Esposito

John L. Esposito is a professor at Georgetown University. He is the author of more than a dozen books on Islam.

In the following excerpt, Esposito traces the rise of Osama bin Laden and his al Qaeda organization following the withdrawal of Soviet troops from Afghanistan in 1989 after a disastrous ten-year occupation. Returning home, the victorious Islamic warriors—mujahideen—who had battled the Soviets sought to spark Islamic revolutions in their own countries. Due to his wealth, family connections, and business skills, Bin Laden was in a good position to bring the dream of Islamic revolution to reality. Esposito explains Bin Laden's activities in the 1990s, first in Sudan, then in Afghanistan, and how Bin Laden's money and know-how were used to establish terrorist bases and train operatives who would wage holy war in the name of Islam.

❧ ❧ ❧

John L. Esposito, *Unholy War: Terror in the Name of Islam*. Oxford, UK: Oxford University Press, 2002. Copyright © 2002 by John L. Esposito. Reproduced by permission of Oxford University Press.

Ⓗow did Osama bin Laden, member of the Saudi elite, mujahid, and hero of the war in Afghanistan, become radicalized? After Soviet troops withdrew from Afghanistan in 1989, bin Laden returned to Saudi Arabia and a job in the family business. Though initially received as a hero, speaking at mosques and to private gatherings, he was soon at loggerheads with the royal family, vociferous in his warning of an impending Iraqi invasion of Kuwait. Saudi Arabia, along with Kuwait and the United States, had for many years, in particular during the Iraq-Iran War [an eight-year war during the 1980s between Saddam Hussein's Iraq and the Islamic Republic of Iran], been strong supporters of Saddam Hussein's Iraq, seeing it as a check on the Ayatollah Khomeini's Iran. When Iraq did invade Kuwait in August 1990, bin Laden quickly wrote to King Fahd, offering to bring the Arab Afghan mujahidin to Saudi Arabia to defend the kingdom. Instead, the deafening silence from the palace was shattered by news that American forces were to defend the House of Saud [the royal family that rules Saudi Arabia]. The admission and stationing of foreign non-Muslim troops in Islam's holy land and their permanent deployment after the Gulf war, bin Laden would later say, transformed his life completely, placing him on a collision course with the Saudi government and the West. He spoke out forcefully against the Saudi alliance with the United States, obtained a *fatwa* (legal opinion) from a senior religious scholar that training was a religious duty, and sent several thousand volunteers to train in Afghanistan.

Like other Arab Afghans [the name for Arabs who fought the Soviet invasion of Afghanistan] who returned to their home countries, in Afghanistan bin Laden had enjoyed the freedom to think and act and to engage in a religious mission to overcome injustice and create an Islamic state and society. In Saudi Arabia he found himself bound within the confines of a regime whose policies and alliances he more and more came to despise as corrupt and un-Islamic. While many of the Arab Afghans who returned to Egypt, Algeria, and elsewhere quickly became involved in radical opposition movements, bin Laden continued to struggle within the system. The government restricted his movement in an attempt to silence him. Finally, in April 1991 he escaped to Afghanistan via Pakistan. When he arrived, however, he found himself not in the Islamic state for which the jihad had been fought but in one mired in the religious and ethnic warfare of its aftermath.

Within a brief period after the Soviet withdrawal, the great Islamic victory had collapsed into interethnic and sectarian warfare, fueled by foreign patrons. The net result was chaos and the devastation of Afghanistan as various warlords vied to set up their own fiefdoms.

Despite the Afghan victory, the jihad had failed to develop a coherent ideology or basis for political unity. The United States walked away from an Afghanistan whose countryside was devastated by a ten-year Soviet occupation that had cost more than one million lives. Mujahidin groups, many of which today [2002] make up the Northern Alliance that with U.S. backing fought and defeated the Taliban, represented competing ethnic, tribal, and religious groups. The country was gripped by a civil war that pitted the majority Pashtun population in the south and east against the ethnic minorities of the north—Tajik, Uzbek, Hazara, and Turkmen. The conflict was further compounded by the intervention and competing agendas of outside powers. Pakistan and Saudi Arabia supported Sunni mujahidin groups while Iran backed an alliance of Shii minority organizations [Sunni and Shii are separate Muslim sects]. The majority of Afghans found themselves caught in the middle of a prolonged civil war marked by heavy fighting, lawlessness, pillaging, rape, and plunder. Bin Laden was frustrated by his inability to contribute to the resolution of the problems of chaos and lawlessness. In 1992, after several months amidst the inter-mujahidin squabbling and fighting over succession after the collapse of the pro-Soviet regime, bin Laden moved to Sudan.

Bin Laden Prospers in Sudan

In January 1989, in a coup led by Colonel Omar al-Bashir, the National Islamic Front (NIF) had come to power in Sudan and established an Islamic republic. Bashir had enlisted the help of Hasan al-Turabi, the Sorbonne-educated leader of the NIF, regarded by many as one of the most brilliant and articulate of the Islamic activist leaders of political Islam internationally. Al-Turabi became the ideologue of the regime, holding a number of political positions, including speaker of the parliament. NIF members provided the backbone and infrastructure for the new government. The government, in a relationship that proved mutually beneficial, welcomed bin Laden. Bin Laden found a refuge and invested his wealth in much-needed construction projects as well as farms and other businesses in the fledgling Islamic state. During these years Sudan, with its open borders, was increasingly condemned by America and Europe for its links with revolutionary Iran and for harboring international terrorists and their training camps. In 1993 Sudan was placed on the State Department's list of countries that sponsor terrorism. Bin Laden was among those individuals whom U.S. intelligence identified as sponsoring terrorist training camps. Although he denied direct involvement and was never formally indicted, bin Laden voiced his approval for the World Trade Center bombing in 1993 and the killing of U.S. troops in Mogadishu, Somalia. American officials were divided as to whether he provided training and arms to those responsible.

Bin Laden's final break with Saudi Arabia came in 1994 when the Kingdom revoked his citizenship and moved to freeze his assets in Saudi Arabia because of his support for fundamentalist movements. From that point on, bin Laden became more outspoken in his denunciation of the House of Saud. Now pushed to the fringe, he joined with other dissident activists and religious scholars to create the Advice and Reform Committee, founded in Saudi Arabia but forced subsequently to move to London. This political opposition group strongly criticized the Saudi regime but did not overtly advocate violence.

By 1995, a series of events and accusations had catapulted the previously obscure bin Laden to center stage. U.S. intelligence sources claimed that he had established extensive training operations in northern Yemen near the Saudi border. Investigators charged that Ramzi Yousef, the captured mastermind of the World Trade Center bombing, had stayed at a bin Laden–financed guesthouse and had financial links to bin Laden. Bin Laden sent a letter to King Fahd advocating guerrilla attacks to drive the U.S. forces out of the Kingdom. Some charged that he was linked to an unsuccessful assassination attempt in Addis Ababa, in June 1995, against President Hosni Mubarak of Egypt. When five Americans and two Indians were killed in a truck bombing in Riyadh in November 1995, bin Laden denied involvement but praised those who committed the attack. Responding to mounting international pressure, especially from the United States and Saudi Arabia, in May 1996 Sudan expelled bin Laden. Ironically, Sudan offered to extradite him to Saudi Arabia or America; both refused to take him. Though some had urged the United States to take advantage of the

tentative overtures that the NIF government was making, the Clinton administration chose otherwise.

Bin Laden fled back to Afghanistan. Shortly after, in
June, a large truck bomb tore apart the Khobar Towers,
a U.S. military residence in Dhahran, Saudi Arabia,
killing nineteen servicemen. Investigators were initially
divided between placing the blame with bin Laden or
with a militant Saudi Shii organization. Bin Laden
praised those behind the Riyadh and Dhahran bombings but denied direct involvement: "I have great respect for the people who did this. What they did is a big
honor that I missed participating in." In June 2001 thirteen members of Saudi Hizbollah, a Shiite group from
the Eastern province of Saudi Arabia, were indicted in
the United States for the Dhahran bombing.

Bin Laden and the Taliban

In 1996, Afghanistan witnessed the rise of an improba-
ble militia that would go on to unite 90 percent of the
country and declare the Islamic Republic of Afghanistan. After almost eighteen years of Soviet occupation
followed by civil war, a seemingly endless cycle of carnage and chaos was abruptly reversed by the astonish-
ing success of a new Islamic movement.

Late in 1994, as if out of nowhere, the predominantly
Pashtun Taliban, a band of *madrasa* (seminary) students
(*taliban*) who had been living as refugees in Pakistan
suddenly appeared. Initially the Taliban were portrayed
as having no military background. In fact many of their
mullahs (religious leaders) and students were veterans of
the Afghan-Soviet war who had returned to the madrasas after the departure of the Soviets. Within two
years they swept across the country, overwhelming the
Northern Alliance of non-Pashtun minorities. Denouncing the contending mujahidin militias, the Taliban claimed the mantle of moral leadership as repre-

sentatives of the majority of Afghans who were victims of the internecine warfare.

At first the Taliban were hailed as liberators who promised to restore law and order, stability and security, and make the streets safe for ordinary citizens. They disarmed the population, cleaned up corruption and graft, and imposed *Shariah* (Islamic law). Initially, they enjoyed success and popularity as a reform movement. It was not until their capture of Kabul [the capital of Afghanistan] in 1996 that they revealed their intention to rule the country and to impose a strict puritanical form of Islam. With substantial support from Saudi Arabia and Pakistan, by 1998 they had subdued 90 percent of the country and driven the Northern Alliance into a small area of northeast Afghanistan.

The Taliban brand of Islamic radicalism has been significantly influenced by a militant neo-Deobandi [Islamic reform] movement in Pakistan. Ironically, the Sunni Deobandi began in the Indian subcontinent as a reformist movement. However, its political expression and ideology were transformed within Pakistan's Jamiyyat-i-Ulama-i-Islam (JUI), a religious party with a rigid, militant, anti-American, and anti-non-Muslim culture. Many of the Taliban were trained in the hundreds of JUI madrasas. Often run by semiliterate mullahs, these schools were first set up for Afghan refugees in the Pashtun-dominated areas of Pakistan, along the border with Afghanistan. Many were supported by Saudi funding that brought with it the influence of an ultraconservative Wahhabi Islam. Students received free education, religious, ideological, and military training. The Taliban teachers showed little knowledge or appreciation for their classical Islamic tradition or for currents of Islamic thought in the broader Muslim world today. They espoused a myopic, self-contained, militant worldview in which Islam is used to legitimate their tribal customs and preferences. The classical Islamic belief in jihad as a defense of Islam and the Muslim community against aggression was transformed into a militant jihad culture and worldview that targets unbelievers, including Muslims and non-Muslims alike.

When they came to power, the Taliban turned over many of their training camps to JUI factions, who in turn trained thousands of Pakistani and Arab militants as well as fighters from South and Central Asia and the Arab world in their radical jihad ideology and tactics. Assisted by military support from Pakistan and financial support from the Wahhabi in Saudi Arabia, with JUI mentoring and influenced by Osama bin Laden's evolving radical jihadist political vision, the Taliban promoted their own brand of revolutionary Islam. They imposed their strict Wahhabi-like brand of Islam on Afghan society. They banned women from school and the workplace, required that men wear beards and women *chadors*, banned music, photography, and television, and imposed strict physical punishments on deviators. Their intolerance for any deviation from their brand of Islam expressed itself in the slaughter of many of Afghanistan's Shii minority (10 percent of the population), whom they disdained as heretics, when the Taliban overran Shii areas such as Mazar-e Sharif in northwest Afghanistan.

Many Muslim religious leaders around the world denounced Taliban "Islamic" policies as aberrant. Muslim governments as diverse as Iran and Egypt, along with Western governments and international human rights organizations, condemned Taliban violations of human rights. Despite their control of most of Afghanistan, by the fall of 1998, neither the United Nations nor most of the global community acknowledged their legitimacy. The Taliban government was recognized by only three nations, Saudi Arabia, Pakistan, and the United Arab Emirates.

Nevertheless, bin Laden found the Taliban's Afghanistan a comfortable haven and useful base of operations. The Taliban leader, Mullah Omar, had been quick to offer sanctuary and express his admiration for bin Laden's sacrifices and dedication to jihad. Bin Laden skillfully cultivated and developed his relationship with Mullah Omar and the Taliban, providing financial support, building roads and other construction projects, and sending his Afghan Arabs to fight alongside the Taliban in critical battles.

Bin Laden's entourage and followers grew steadily. He attracted Arab and other Muslim dissidents, many of whom had had to flee their native countries. Among them were several prominent Egyptian radicals: Dr. Ayman al-Zawahiri, a physician and a leader of the banned Islamic Jihad in Egypt; Rifai Taha Musa, leader of Egypt's banned Gamaa Islamiyya; and two sons of Shaykh Omar Abdel Rahman, the blind Egyptian preacher indicted for involvement in the assassination of [Egyptian president] Anwar Sadat, suspected of involvement in the World Trade Center bombing of 1993, and later found guilty of conspiring to blow up major sites in New York City. Omar Abdel Rahman had visited Afghanistan several times during the war against the Soviets, when he and bin Laden had first met. Of these men, however, the one to wield the most influence over bin Laden would be Dr. Ayman al-Zawahiri.

Ayman al-Zawahiri: Bin Laden's Right-Hand Man

The story of Ayman al-Zawahiri is that of a gifted surgeon who became a leader of an Egyptian terrorist group on the road to becoming Osama bin Laden's confidant, reputed mentor, and successor. Ayman al-Zawahiri was born in 1953 into a prominent and conservative religious family. He grew up in Maadi, an upscale suburb of Cairo inhabited by wealthy Egyptians and foreign diplomats. His grandfathers were the rector of al-Azhar University, the Islamic world's oldest and most prestigious religious school, and president of Cairo University, Egypt's leading modern secular university.

Family and friends remember Ayman as a normal, well-adjusted young man—an intelligent, well-read, polite student who went on to become a physician. However, 1967 had been a defining moment for him as it was for many in the Arab world. After the disastrous Arab defeat in the 1967 Arab-Israeli (Six Day) war and the disillusionment over Arab (secular) nationalism and socialism that followed, al-Zawahiri turned to political Islam. He joined the Muslim Brotherhood [a long-established group seeking to impose Islamic law in Egypt] when he was only fourteen years old. By 1979, he had embraced a radical option and joined Islamic Jihad, a violent extremist group composed of small clandestine cells. He quickly became one of its leaders and by 1983 was recruiting members, organizing secret cells and underground operations. After the assassination of Anwar Sadat, Zawahiri was arrested along with hundreds of others. Though no direct link to Sadat's death could be established, he was tried and sentenced to three years in prison on charges of possessing weapons. After his 1984 release from prison, where like many others he had been beaten and tortured, he briefly returned to medical practice in a clinic. The political climate in Egypt and his radical past and prison record, however, prompted al-Zawahiri to emigrate and take a position in Saudi Arabia. Within the year he went to Afghanistan, where he worked as a surgeon, treating wounded Afghan and Arab fighters in field hospitals. It was during this time that he met Dr. Abdullah Azzam, the Palestinian Islamist activist who had taught bin Laden at King Abdulaziz University in Jeddah, Saudi Arabia. Azzam had gone to Pakistan to make his contribution to the war in Afghanistan. After a short stint teaching at the Islamic University in Islamabad, Pakistan, he founded the Jihad Service Bureau, whose mission was the recruitment of Saudis and other Arabs through publications and other media. Azzam joined with bin Laden and Zawahiri in recruiting and training Muslims for the jihad against the Soviets. They formed a lasting friendship and alliance in their growing commitment to a global jihad. After the Soviet defeat in 1989, Zawahiri returned to Egypt and to his leadership role in Islamic Jihad.

Zawahiri played an important role during the 1990s, organizing underground operations and integrating former mujahidin into the ranks of Islamic Jihad. The violence and terrorism of Islamic Jihad were met with equal force by Egyptian military and police. Bloody confrontations were accompanied by the arrest, interrogation, torture, and imprisonment of thousands.

In 1992 Zawahiri moved to Sudan with bin Laden, and in 1996 both returned to Afghanistan. From there, al-Zawahiri continued to be involved in the jihad against the Egyptian state. He is believed to have been the mastermind behind terrorist attacks, including the massacre of fifty-eight tourists in Luxor in 1997, for which he was sentenced to death in absentia by an Egyptian court in 1999. He also merged Islamic Jihad with al-Qaeda and worked with Osama bin Laden to plot and execute their global jihad. Many believed that Zawahiri possessed a deeper theological understanding and more international perspective than bin Laden, and that he was responsible for broadening bin Laden's vista for jihad beyond the Arab world to the wider Muslim world and to a jihad against America and/or the West. Hamid Mir, a Pakistani journalist who interviewed bin Laden, believes that al-Zawahiri also masterminded the September 11, 2001, attacks. Although only religious leaders can legitimately issue fatwas, bin Laden had nevertheless issued a fatwa allowing the killing of innocent people: "to kill Americans and their allies—civilians and military—is an individual duty for every Muslim who can do it in any country in which it is possible to do it." When Mir pressed him on how this was permissible in light of the fact that the Prophet Muhammad forbade Muslims to kill innocent civilians, he noted that bin Laden responded only after consulting with Zawahiri and checking some Islamic sources. Others, however, contend that bin Laden has long had a global animosity toward America and Israel as well as the intellectual and financial means to pursue it, and that it is he who broadened the perspective of Zawahiri, who had spent the bulk of his formative years as a terrorist focused on toppling the regime and establishing an Islamic state in Egypt. Regardless of who influenced whom, the bin Laden and Zawahiri joint venture produced a powerful global ideology and agenda.

Bin Laden Speaks About His Plans for an Islamic Revolution

Peter L. Bergen

In 1997 American journalist Peter L. Bergen was approached by a representative of Osama bin Laden. Bin Laden had apparently decided that Bergen's employer, the Cable News Network (CNN), was the best forum for spreading his message of jihad against the United States. With the help of a guide, Bergen and his colleague Peter Arnett traveled to Afghanistan and made contact with Bin Laden. During the interview, Bin Laden stated his goal of uniting the Muslim *umma*, or community of believers, through jihad—holy war. He made clear his grievance against the United States. He proclaimed his hatred of the government of his home country, Saudi Arabia, which he saw as a puppet of America. He also denounced Israel and its treatment of the Palestinians. Bin Laden announced his intention to fight the United States and Israel by attacking both military and civilian targets.

Peter L. Bergen, *Holy War, Inc.: Inside the Secret World of Osama bin Laden*. London: Weidenfeld & Nicolson, 2001. Copyright © 2001 by Peter L. Bergen. Reproduced by permission of Weidenfeld & Nicolson, an imprint of the Orion Publishing Group.

I calculated that it was some time before midnight when bin Laden appeared with his entourage—a translator and several bodyguards. He is a tall man, well over six feet, his face dominated by an aquiline nose. Dressed in a turban, white robes, and a green camouflage jacket, he walked with a cane and seemed tired, less like a swaggering revolutionary than a Muslim ascetic [hermit]. Those around him treated him with the utmost deference, referring to him with the honorific 'sheikh', a homage he seemed to take as his due. We were told we had about an hour with him before he would have to go. As he sat down, he propped up next to him the Kalashnikov rifle that is never far from his side. His followers said he had taken it from a Russian he had killed.

[Cameraman Peter] Jouvenal fiddled with the lights and camera and then said the welcome words 'We have speed,' which is cameramanese for 'We're ready.'

Peter Arnett [Bergen's colleague at CNN] and I had worked up a long list of questions, many more than could be answered in the hour allotted to us. We had been asked to submit them in advance, and bin Laden's people had excised any questions about his personal life, his family, or his finances. We were not going to find out, Barbara Walters–style, what kind of tree bin Laden thought he was. But he was going to answer our questions about his political views and why he advocated violence against Americans.

Bin Laden Denounces the United States

Without raising his voice, bin Laden began to rail in Arabic against the injustices visited upon Muslims by the United States and his native Saudi Arabia: 'Our main problem is the US government. . . . By being loyal to the US regime, the Saudi regime has committed an act against Islam,' he said. Bin Laden made no secret of the fact that he was interested in fomenting a revolution in Saudi Arabia, and that his new regime would rule in accordance with the seventh-century precepts of the Prophet Muhammad. 'We are confident . . . that Muslims will be victorious in the Arabian peninsula and that God's religion, praise and glory be to Him, will prevail in this peninsula. It is a great . . . hope that the revelation unto Muhammad will be used for ruling.'

Bin Laden coughed softly throughout the interview and nursed a cup of tea. No doubt he was suffering from a cold brought on by the draughty Afghan mountains. He continued on in his soft-spoken but focused manner, an ambiguous, thin smile sometimes playing on his lips: 'We declared jihad against the US government because the US government . . . has committed acts that are extremely unjust, hideous, and criminal whether directly or through its support of the Israeli occupation of [Palestine]. And we believe the US is directly responsible for those who were killed in Palestine, Lebanon, and Iraq. This US government abandoned humanitarian feelings by these hideous crimes. It transgressed all bounds and behaved in a way not witnessed before by any power or any imperialist power in the world. Due to its subordination to the Jews, the arrogance and haughtiness of the US regime has reached to the extent that they occupied [Arabia]. For this and other acts of aggression and injustice, we have declared jihad [holy war] against the US, because in our religion it is our duty to make jihad so that God's word is the one exalted to the heights and so that we drive the Americans away from all Muslim countries.'

Throughout bin Laden's diatribe perhaps a dozen of his followers listened in rapt attention as he went on to clarify that the call for jihad was directed against US armed forces stationed in the Saudi Kingdom.

A Threat to Attack US Forces in Saudi Arabia

'We have focused our declaration on striking at the soldiers in the country of the Two Holy Places.' This was bin Laden's name for Saudi Arabia, a term he avoids using, as he loathes the Saudi royal family.

He continued: 'The country of the Two Holy Places has in our religion a peculiarity of its own over the other Muslim countries. In our religion, it is not permissible for any non-Muslim to stay in our country. Therefore, even though American civilians are not targeted in our plan, they must leave. We do not guarantee their safety.'

This was the first time that bin Laden had told members of the Western press that American civilians might be casualties in his holy war. A year later he would tell ABC News that he made no distinction between American military and civilian targets, despite the fact that the Koran itself is explicit about the protections offered to civilians.

Bin Laden went on to say that the end of the Cold War had made the United States overreach: 'The collapse of the Soviet Union made the US more haughty and arrogant and it has started to look at itself as a master of this world and established what it calls the New World Order.'

Terrorists Benefit from Technology

It was ironic that bin Laden was critical of the post–Cold War environment. It was precisely the end of the Cold War, which brought more open borders, that allowed his organization to flourish. According to the US indictment against him, his network had established cells in twenty countries during the 1990s. Some of those countries, such as Croatia, Bosnia, Tajikistan, and Azerbaijan, owed their very existence to the end of the Cold War. And bin Laden represented a shift in the way terrorists operated, a shift made possible by the changing rules of the New World Order. While bin Laden transferred his millions from Saudi Arabia to Sudan to Afghanistan, his followers enthusiastically embraced the artifacts of globalization. They communicated by American satellite phones and kept their plans on Japanese-made computers. Bin Laden's *fatwas* [religious rulings] were faxed to other countries, particularly England, where Arabic-language newspapers reprinted them and transmitted them throughout the Middle East. Thus was bin Laden able to create a truly global network.

Bin Laden's Goal Is to Unify All Muslims

Bin Laden envisaged his own counterpoint to the march of globalization—the restoration of the *Khalifa*, or caliphate, which would begin from Afghanistan. Not since the final demise of the Ottoman Empire [an Islamic empire based in what is now Turkey] after the end of World War I had there been a Muslim entity that more or less united the *umma*, the community of Muslim believers, under the green flag of Islam. In this view, the treaties that followed World War I had carved up the Ottoman Empire, 'the Sick Man of Europe', into ersatz entities like Iraq and Syria. Bin Laden aimed to create the conditions for the rebirth of the *Khalifa*, where the *umma* would live under the rule of the Prophet Muhammad in a continuous swath of green from Tunisia to Indonesia, much as the red of the British empire colored maps from Egypt to Burma before World War II. As a practical matter, the restoration of the *Khalifa* had about as much chance as the Holy Roman Empire suddenly reappearing in Europe, but as a rhetorical device the call for its return exercised a powerful grip on bin Laden and his followers.

During the interview bin Laden's translator, who spoke precise English, gave us rough translations of what bin

Laden was saying. Occasionally, though, bin Laden would answer questions before they had been translated. So he clearly understood some English. 'The US today has set a double standard, calling whoever goes against its injustice a terrorist,' he said at one point. 'It wants to occupy our countries, steal our resources, impose on us agents to rule us . . . and wants us to agree to all these. If we refuse to do so, it will say, "You are terrorists." With a simple look at the US behaviors, we find that it judges the behavior of the poor Palestinian children whose country was occupied: if they throw stones against the Israeli occupation, it says they are terrorists, whereas when the Israeli pilots bombed the United Nations building in Qana, Lebanon, while it was full of children and women, the US stopped any plan to condemn Israel.' (This was a reference to 18 April 1996, when Israeli forces seeking to attack Hezbollah guerrillas shelled a UN building in Qana, Lebanon, killing 102 Lebanese civilians. Israel characterized the attack on the UN building as an accident, a claim the UN later dismissed.)

Bin Laden angrily continued. 'At the same time that they condemn any Muslim who calls for his rights, they receive the top official of the Irish Republican Army [Gerry Adams] at the White House as a political leader. Wherever we look, we find the US as the leader of terrorism and crime in the world. The US does not consider it a terrorist act to throw atomic bombs at nations thousands of miles away, when those bombs would hit more than just military targets. Those bombs rather were thrown at entire nations, including women, children, and elderly people, and up to this day the traces of those bombs remain in Japan.'

Killing US Troops in Somalia

Bin Laden then surprised us by claiming that Arabs affiliated with his group were involved in killing American troops in Somalia in 1993, a claim he had earlier made to an Arabic newspaper. We all remembered the grisly television images of the mutilated body of a US serviceman being dragged through the streets of Mogadishu. What was not known at the time was the possible involvement of bin Laden's organization in training the Somalis who carried out the operation.

Bin Laden told us: 'Resistance started against the American invasion, because Muslims did not believe the US allegations that they came to save the Somalis. With Allah's grace, Muslims in Somalia cooperated with some Arab holy warriors who were in Afghanistan. Together they killed large numbers of American occupation troops.' For bin Laden, Somalia was clearly an intoxicating victory. He exulted in the fact that the United States withdrew its troops from the country, pointing to the withdrawal as an example of the 'weakness, frailty and cowardice of the US troops.'

Asked what message he would send President Clinton, bin Laden answered: 'Mentioning the name of Clinton or that of the American government provokes disgust and revulsion. This is because the name of the American government and the name of Clinton and Bush directly reflect in our minds . . . the picture of the children who died in Iraq.' He was referring to the fact that, by May 1996, an estimated 500,000 Iraqi children had died as a result of UN sanctions imposed on Iraq in 1990, for its continued violations of UN resolutions.

He continued: 'The hearts of Muslims are filled with hatred towards the United States of America and the American president. The president has a heart that knows no words. A heart that kills hundreds of children definitely knows no words. Our people in the Arabian Peninsula will send him messages with no words because he does not know any words. If there is a message that I may send through you, then it is a message I address to the mothers of the American troops who came here with their military uniforms walking proudly up and down our land. . . . I say that this represents a blatant provocation to over a billion Muslims. To these mothers I say, if they are concerned for their sons, then let them object to the American government's policy.'

An Ominous Warning

The interview came to an end, but bin Laden lingered for a few minutes, courteously serving us cups of tea. The talk turned to Iraq and Saddam Hussein, whom Arnett had interviewed during the Gulf War. Bin Laden said that the Iraqi dictator wanted the oil of Kuwait for his own aggrandizement and was not a true Muslim leader.

After posing for a couple of photos, bin Laden left as quickly as he had arrived. He had spent a little over an hour with us. But the 'media adviser' was reluctant to give up the interview tapes. First, he wanted to erase some shots of bin Laden he considered unflattering. With several of bin Laden's guards still present, there was no way to stop him. I watched as he proceeded to erase the offending images by taping over the interview tape inside the camera. Not content with this little display, he then started an argument with Ali [Bergen's guide] about giving us the tapes at all. A tugging match ensued. Finally, Ali prevailed, giving me both interview tapes, which were hardly larger than a pair of matchbooks. I put them in the most secure place I could think of: inside my money belt, which I wore under my trousers.

'Will you use the bit of the interview where bin Laden attacks Clinton?' Ali asked. We were standing outside the mud hut underneath a vast sky. There is no light pollution or smog in Afghanistan, so the heavens can be seen in their natural state. It was a beautiful night, clear and cold and utterly, utterly silent. 'Of course,' I told him. Ali seemed surprised. He was used to firm government control of the media.

During the next weeks we wrote and edited the script for our profile, which was broadcast on 12 May 1997, in the United States and over a hundred other countries. In Saudi Arabia, authorities confiscated copies of newspapers that ran items about our story, while in the US the Associated Press wire service ran a piece that was picked up by a number of American papers. Otherwise, the story had little impact.

But a line kept resonating in my mind, the final words in our broadcast. When asked about his future plans bin Laden had replied:

'You'll see them and hear about them in the media, God willing.'

Bin Laden Rallies the Islamic World After the 9/11 Attacks

Osama bin Laden

After the September 11, 2001, attacks, the United States launched military strikes against Afghanistan, whose ruling Taliban regime was harboring Osama bin Laden and his terrorist camps. During the conflict, the terrorist group al Qaeda released a taped speech of Bin Laden. An excerpt from the transcript of the speech follows.

In the speech, Bin Laden claims the world is divided into two camps. One camp, which he praises, hails the attacks against the United States and condemns the war in Afghanistan. The other camp, which he calls traitors to Islam, denounces the September 11 attacks and supports the war in Afghanistan. He singles out Israel, the United States, and the United Nations as aggressors and vows to continue to fight against them.

🌸 🌸 🌸

Osama bin Laden, "Bin Laden Rails Against Crusaders and UN," http://news.bbc.co.uk, November 3, 2001.

Wwe praise God, seek His help, and ask for His for-
giveness.

We seek refuge in God from the evils of our souls
and our bad deeds.

A person who is guided by God will never be misguided by anyone and a person who is misguided by
God can never be guided by anyone.

I bear witness that there is no God but Allah alone,
Who has no partner.

Muslims and Christians Divided

Amid the huge developments and in the wake of the
great strikes that hit the United States in its most important locations in New York and Washington, a huge
media clamour has been raised.

This clamour is unprecedented. It conveyed the
opinions of people on these events.

People were divided into two parts. The first part
supported these strikes against US tyranny, while the
second denounced them.

Afterward, when the United States launched the unjust campaign against the Islamic Emirate in Afghanistan, people also split into two parties.

The first supported these campaigns, while the second denounced and rejected them.

These tremendous incidents, which have split people
into two parties, are of great interest to the Muslims,
since many of the rulings pertain to them.

These rulings are closely related to Islam and the acts
that corrupt a person's Islam.

Therefore, the Muslims must understand the nature
and truth of this conflict so that it will be easy for them
to determine where they stand.

While talking about the truth of the conflict, opinion
polls in the world have shown that a little more than 80

per cent of Westerners, of Christians in the United States and elsewhere, have been saddened by the strikes that hit the United States.

The polls showed that the vast majority of the sons of the Islamic world were happy about these strikes because they believe that the strikes were in reaction to the huge criminality practiced by Israel and the United States in Palestine and other Muslim countries.

After the strikes on Afghanistan began, these groups changed positions.

Those who were happy about striking the United States felt sad when Afghanistan was hit, and those who felt sad when the United States was hit were happy when Afghanistan was hit. These groups comprise millions of people.

Support in the Islamic World

The entire West, with the exception of a few countries, supports this unfair, barbaric campaign, although there is no evidence of the involvement of the people of Afghanistan in what happened in America.

The people of Afghanistan had nothing to do with this matter. The campaign, however, continues to unjustly annihilate the villagers and civilians, children, women, and innocent people.

The positions of the two sides are very clear. Mass demonstrations have spread from the farthest point in the eastern part of the Islamic world to the farthest point in the western part of the Islamic world, and from Indonesia, Philippines, Bangladesh, India, Pakistan to the Arab world and Nigeria and Mauritania.

War "Fundamentally Religious"

This clearly indicates the nature of this war. This war is fundamentally religious. The people of the East are Muslims. They sympathized with Muslims against the people of the West, who are the crusaders.

Those who try to cover this crystal clear fact, which the entire world has admitted, are deceiving the Islamic nation.

They are trying to deflect the attention of the Islamic nation from the truth of this conflict.

This fact is proven in the book of God Almighty and in the teachings of our messenger, may God's peace and blessings be upon him.

Under no circumstances should we forget this enmity between us and the infidels. For, the enmity is based on creed.

We must be loyal to the believers and those who believe that there is no God but Allah.

We should also renounce the atheists and infidels. It suffices me to seek God's help against them.

God says: "Never will the Jews or the Christians be satisfied with thee unless thou follow their form of religion."

It is a question of faith, not a war against terrorism, as Bush and Blair try to depict it.

Many thieves belonging to this nation were captured in the past. But, nobody moved.

The masses which moved in the East and West have not done so for the sake of Osama.

Rather, they moved for the sake of their religion. This is because they know that they are right and that they resist the most ferocious, serious, and violent Crusade campaign against Islam ever since the message was revealed to Muhammad, may God's peace and blessings be upon him.

After this has become clear, the Muslim must know and learn where he is standing vis-a-vis this war.

United States Provokes Hatred
After the US politicians spoke and after the US newspapers and television channels became full of clear cru-

sading hatred in this campaign that aims at mobilizing the West against Islam and Muslims, Bush left no room for doubts or the opinions of journalists, but he openly and clearly said that this war is a crusader war. He said this before the whole world to emphasize this fact.

What can those who allege that this is a war against terrorism say? What terrorism are they speaking about at a time when the Islamic nation has been slaughtered for tens of years without hearing their voices and without seeing any action by them?

But when the victim starts to take revenge for those innocent children in Palestine, Iraq, southern Sudan, Somalia, Kashmir [a province in northern India] and the Philippines, the rulers' ulema (Islamic leaders) and the hypocrites come to defend the clear blasphemy. It suffices me to seek God's help against them.

The common people have understood the issue, but there are those who continue to flatter those who colluded with the unbelievers to anesthetize the Islamic nation to prevent it from carrying out the duty of jihad so that the word of God will be above all words.

The unequivocal truth is that Bush has carried the cross and raised its banner high and stood at the front of the queue.

Anyone who lines up behind Bush in this campaign has committed one of the 10 actions that sully one's Islam.

Muslim scholars are unanimous that allegiance to the infidels and support for them against the believers is one of the major acts that sully Islam.

Muslims Are Attacked by "Crusaders"

There is no power but in God. Let us investigate whether this war against Afghanistan that broke out a few days ago is a single and unique one or if it is a link to a long series of crusader wars against the Islamic world.

Following World War I, which ended more than 83

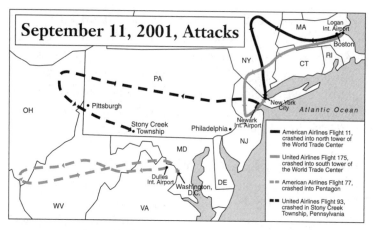

September 11, 2001, Attacks

American Airlines Flight 11, crashed into north tower of the World Trade Center

United Airlines Flight 175, crashed into south tower of the World Trade Center

American Airlines Flight 77, crashed into Pentagon

United Airlines Flight 93, crashed in Stony Creek Township, Pennsylvania

years ago, the whole Islamic world fell under the crusader banner—under the British, French, and Italian governments.

They divided the whole world, and Palestine was occupied by the British.

Since then, and for more than 83 years, our brothers, sons, and sisters in Palestine have been badly tortured.

Hundreds of thousands of them have been killed, and hundreds of thousands of them have been imprisoned or maimed.

Let us examine the recent developments. Take for example the Chechens [a people living in the south of Russia].

They are a Muslim people who have been attacked by the Russian bear which embraces the Christian Orthodox faith.

Russians have annihilated the Chechen people in their entirety and forced them to flee to the mountains where they were assaulted by snow and poverty and diseases.

Nonetheless, nobody moved to support them. There is no strength but in God.

This was followed by a war of genocide in Bosnia in sight and hearing of the entire world in the heart of Europe.

For several years our brothers have been killed, our women have been raped, and our children have been massacred in the safe havens of the United Nations and with its knowledge and cooperation.

Those who refer our tragedies today to the United Nations so that they can be resolved are hypocrites who deceive God, His Prophet and the believers.

The United Nations Colludes with the West

Are not our tragedies but caused by the United Nations? Who issued the Partition Resolution on Palestine in 1947 and surrendered the land of Muslims to the Jews? It was the United Nations in its resolution in 1947.

Those who claim that they are the leaders of the Arabs and continue to appeal to the United Nations have disavowed what was revealed to Prophet Muhammad, God's peace and blessings be upon him.

Those who refer things to the international legitimacy have disavowed the legitimacy of the Holy Book and the tradition of Prophet Muhammad, God's peace and blessings be upon him.

This is the United Nations from which we have suffered greatly. Under no circumstances should any Muslim or sane person resort to the United Nations. The United Nations is nothing but a tool of crime.

We are being massacred everyday, while the United Nations continues to sit idly by.

A Series of Conspiracies Against Islam

Our brothers in Kashmir have been subjected to the worst forms of torture for over 50 years. They have been massacred, killed, and raped. Their blood has been shed and their houses have been trespassed upon.

Still, the United Nations continues to sit idly by.

Today, and without any evidence, the United Nations passes resolutions supporting unjust and tyrannical America, which oppresses these helpless people who have emerged from a merciless war at the hands of the Soviet Union.

Let us look at the second war in Chechnya, which is still underway. The entire Chechen people are being embattled once again by this Russian bear.

The humanitarian agencies, even the US ones, demanded that President Clinton should stop supporting Russia.

However, Clinton said that stopping support for Russia did not serve US interests.

[In 2002, Russian president Vladimir] Putin demanded that the cross and the Jews should stand by him. He told them: You must support us and thank us because we are waging a war against Muslim fundamentalism.

The enemies are speaking very clearly. While this is taking place, the leaders of the region hide and are ashamed to support their brothers.

Let us examine the stand of the West and the United Nations in the developments in Indonesia when they moved to divide the largest country in the Islamic world in terms of population.

This criminal, [UN general secretary] Kofi Annan, was speaking publicly and putting pressure on the Indonesian government, telling it: You have 24 hours to divide and separate East Timor [a Christian part of predominately Muslim Indonesia] from Indonesia.

Otherwise, we will be forced to send in military forces to separate it by force.

The crusader Australian forces were on Indonesian shores, and in fact they landed to separate East Timor, which is part of the Islamic world.

Therefore, we should view events not as separate links, but as links in a long series of conspiracies, a war of annihilation in the true sense of the word.

In Somalia, on the excuse of restoring hope, 13,000

of our brothers were killed. In southern Sudan, hundreds of thousands were killed.

Muslims Cannot Tolerate Attacks on Palestinians

But when we move to Palestine and Iraq, there can be no bounds to what can be said.

Over one million children were killed in Iraq. The killing is continuing.

As for what is taking place in Palestine these days, I can only say we have no one but God to complain to.

What is taking place cannot be tolerated by any nation. I do not say from the nations of the human race, but from other creatures, from the animals. They would not tolerate what is taking place.

A confidant of mine told me that he saw a butcher slaughtering a camel in front of another camel.

The other camel got agitated while seeing the blood coming out of the other camel. Thus, it burst out with rage and bit the hand of the man and broke it.

How can the weak mothers in Palestine endure the killing of their children in front of their eyes by the unjust Jewish executioners with US support and with US aircraft and tanks?

Those who distinguish between America and Israel are the real enemies of the nation. They are traitors who betrayed God and His Prophet, and who betrayed their nation and the trust placed in them. They anesthetize the nation.

These battles cannot be viewed in any case whatsoever as isolated battles, but rather, as part of a chain of the long, fierce, and ugly crusader war.

Words of the Prophet Muhammad

Every Muslim must stand under the banner of There is no God but Allah and Muhammad is God's Prophet.

I remind you of what our Prophet, may God's peace and blessings be upon him, told Ibn Abbas, may God be pleased with him.

He told him: Boy, I am going to teach you a few words. Obey God, He will protect you. Obey Him, you will find Him on your side. If you ask for something, ask God. If you seek help, seek the help of God.

You should know that if all people come together to help you, they will only help you with something that God has already preordained for you.

And if they assemble to harm you, they will only harm you with something that God has already preordained for you. God wrote man's fate and it will never change.

I tell the Muslims who did their utmost during these weeks: You must continue along the same march.

Your support for us will make us stronger and will further support your brothers in Afghanistan.

Exert more efforts in combating this unprecedented war crime.

Fear God, O Muslims and rise to support your religion. Islam is calling on you: O Muslims, O Muslims, O Muslims.

God bear witness that I have conveyed the message.
God bear witness that I have conveyed the message.
God bear witness that I have conveyed the message.
God's peace and blessings be upon you.

Profiles · in · History

Dictators and State Terror

Maximilien Robespierre and the Reign of Terror

Albert Parry

The term *terror*, when used to mean violence for political ends, has origins in the French Revolution. The revolution began in 1789 as a popular uprising against the monarchy, but by 1793 had taken a bloody turn to broad purges of "antirevolutionary" elements in all classes. In April of that year the Committee of Public Safety took control of France by means of mass arrests and executions. More than two hundred thousand French citizens were thrown in jail, and thousands were executed by guillotine. A revolt called the Vendée against this "Reign of Terror" resulted in more executions. In the city of Nantes alone, thirty-five hundred people were killed by drowning in reprisal for rebelling against the revolutionary authorities.

The head of the Committee of Public Safety was Maximilien Robespierre. Robespierre was born in 1758, at Arras, a city in northern France. His grandfather and father had been lawyers, and Maximilien followed them into this profession. He gained a reputation as a radical politician and leader of the Jacobin Party early in the revolution, finally attaining control of the Committee of Public Safety

Albert Parry, *Terrorism: From Robespierre to Arafat*. New York: Vanguard Press, 1976. Copyright © 1976 by Albert Parry. All rights reserved. Reproduced by permission of Random House, Inc.

in 1793. He demanded the death of the deposed king and ruthlessly sent friends to the guillotine.

By 1794 many who had supported the revolution were turning against Robespierre. Fearing he would target them next, members of the French National Convention joined forces to overthrow the rule of the Committee of Public Safety. Robespierre was arrested and executed on July 28, 1794. His Reign of Terror had lasted just a little over a year, but tens of thousands had perished as the result of this first example of state violence on a mass scale.

Biographer Albert Parry has profiled Germany's Baader-Meinhof terrorist gang as well as terrorist leaders from the eighteenth century to the present day. He is also the author of *The Russian Scientist*.

🜚 🜚 🜚

"**H**e will go far because he believes everything he says." This faith in his own verity and honesty was "the secret of his influence." Thus, early in the Revolution, spoke Count Honoré Gabriel de Mirabeau, who until his death in 1791 was himself one of the most prominent men in revolutionary France. The subject of his remarks was Maximilien Robespierre.

Robespierre, born in 1758 to a middle-class French family of Irish extraction, was a frail child in his native town of Arras [about one hundred miles north of Paris]. Going to Paris on a scholarship given him by the bishop of Artois, he proved an exemplary schoolboy at the Collège Louis-le-Grand—studious, gentle, shy. His Jesuit masters loved him, mostly because he was excellent in rhetoric, a skillful orator, though of scant emotionalism.

Later, at the law school of the University of Paris, he was a classmate of Camille Desmoulins, destined to be his fellow revolutionary and one of his many victims.

Returning to Arras to practice law, Robespierre won his very first important case and was appointed a criminal judge, but soon resigned because, he said, he could not bear to hand out death sentences.

At Arras he also indulged himself in literary pretensions, as a dilettante member and director of the Rosati, a society dedicated to the cultivation of wit and letters. In the spirit of his time he composed verses that were remembered as "gallant and Bacchic [frenzied]."

On the serious side he read all of [the Swiss philosopher Jean-Jacques] Rousseau's works religiously, called on the great sage in person, and considered himself a thoroughly understanding and faithful disciple of that philosopher's vision of an ideal society. In 1789, at 30, Robespierre was sent to Paris as an elected deputy to the Estates-General [the prerevolutionary parliament of France]. There, and later in the Constituent Assembly, he gradually lost the last traces of his timidity. Joining extreme radicals, he delivered numerous speeches, evading no issues, hammering the same persistent points again and again. All of his plodding and increasingly fanatical self he put into his oratory, his ideas, his work.

At first some of his colleagues and many of the public laughed at his idealistic theories and personal traits. But he walked and talked through all this as if these jests and insults were of no matter. With his perseverance, his tremendous capacity for work, he was making headway. His frenetic praise of Rousseau helped. As the more conservative of his fellow members in the Jacobin Club [a group of radical revolutionaries] withdrew in 1791, Robespierre became its head. When, in December 1792, [King] Louis XVI was brought to trial at the Convention [the French national assembly during the revolution], it was Robespierre's cold and murderous speech more than any other factor that decided the 387-to-334 vote of death for the King.

A Virtuous Killer

Becoming first among the equals, killing thousands in the name of virtue, Robespierre spoke in sorrow about his own sacrifices and sufferings. Women burst into sobs, and more and more idolizers hailed him as "The Incorruptible," while those close to him called him "kind friend."

In appearance, although he dressed well, he was rather unremarkable. His hair was neatly powdered; his clothes were immaculate, appraised by some connoisseurs as of sober and tasteful elegance, but by others as foppish: knee breeches and silk stockings; a nankin-yellow or blue or brown coat and a chamois waistcoat; and a huge pleated bow tie, arranged with painstaking care to practically smother his neck. Small-statured, his poses unimpressive, his stride jerky, he had a harsh voice. His chin was short and sharp; his skin a sickly yellow. His eyes were piercing but half covered by the eyelids, deep in the sockets. Their look was described as *verdâtre* [greenish], possibly because of his green-tinted spectacles. His fine but small forehead bulged somewhat above his temples. His nose was small, narrow and pointed, but with very wide nostrils; his mouth large but the lips thin, pressed at the corners unpleasantly, with an indecisive smile verging on sarcasm.

He was sparing in his food habits, and walked instead of riding to and from his clean and modest lodgings. These were in the house of the intensely admiring Maurice Duplay, a prosperous and bourgeois but radical-thinking carpenter, who together with his wife and four daughters waited on him as much as he would allow. The girls sometimes played the harpsichord for their illustrious lodger, in the respites between his orations and writing, and his running of France under the giant shadow of the guillotine. Three of the four daughters were unmarried, and one—Eléonore—was particularly worshipful.

Fond of her, he was rumored to be her lover, but in fact (perhaps) was no more than her proper and austere fiancé.

"Sinister sweetness" and "macabre-tragic significance" were among the phrases applied by later historians of the Revolution to Robespierre's figure, face, clothes, and habits.

Robespierre's Rise to Leadership

In the momentous year of 1792 Robespierre, this lawyer who hated law, rose to leadership in the Convention slowly, almost imperceptibly. In July 1793, upon his joining the Committee of Public Safety [the executive committee of the Convention charged with enforcing laws], it was immediately apparent that he was the undisputed chief of the French Revolution. Under him, terror erupted in earnest. His first targets were the Girondins [moderate revolutionaries].

The Girondins, with no true unity among themselves, lacked a definite attitude to terror. On the one hand they publicly deplored the September Massacres,[1] branding them as sheer anarchy, thus confirming the Jacobins in their ardent support for the very same Massacres and so widening the chasm in the Convention and in French revolutionary politics in general. On the other hand, the Girondins, after pleading for a milder sentence for the King, finally voted his death.

But even the execution of Louis XVI in January 1793 did not wholly unleash the historic Terror. The bloody wave rose high beginning in June 1793, when the Girondins were expelled by the Jacobins from the Convention and, in the next few months, were sent by Robespierre to the guillotine. The Jacobins were then aided by that small but virulent club of the Cordeliers [a group

1. The slaughter of imprisoned priests, noblemen, and other "enemies of the revolution" from September 2 to 7, 1792. The killings were carried out by the mobs of Paris, often in an exceptionally brutal manner.

of radical revolutionaries], led by the fiery lawyer [revolutionary leader Georges Jacques] Danton and the flamboyant journalist and orator [Camille] Desmoulins.

The Theory of Terror

As for the theory of terror, it was Danton who, among the first, formulated its purpose: Terror was a most desirable, most urgent weapon to defend the young Republic against its foes, both foreign and domestic. To an extent he was echoed by Lazare Carnot, the revolutionist who had been trained as a military engineer, and who from 1792 on was to go into history as the organizer of the new revolutionary armies of France and the architect of her eventual military victories over the Austrians and other foreign enemies. Carnot proclaimed that the Great Terror was the explanation of these triumphs. In truth, however, the principal successes of the French armies came before, not during, the Terror's sharpest crests. The Great Terror did not inspirit the citizen-soldiers; it frightened not the invaders, but the French themselves.

Danton, in his speech at the chaotic session of the Convention of August 12, 1793, urged, as one of the measures of stepping up the Terror, the arrest—as hostages—of all "suspects" in Paris and the provinces. In the Convention's session of September 5 commemorating the first anniversary of the Massacres, it was decided to expand the Revolutionary Tribunal and to form a special army of 6,000 infantrymen and 1,200 cannoneers to carry terror throughout the nation.

In addition, Danton proposed revolutionizing all worthy men, particularly in Paris, by providing every worker with a rifle. Revolutionaries everywhere were to have arbitrary power to detain, judge, and execute any and all "suspects."

Bertrand Barère, an ardent Jacobin, summarized: "Let us make terror the order of the day!" Terror was not to be an exception to the new life—it was to be its ambiance and prime rule. People would have to accept it for their own welfare. Another Jacobin rationalized: "Since neither our virtue nor our moderation nor our philosophic ideas have been of use to us, let us be brigands for the good of the people." This was the phraseology that would live for generations, and with such pithy excuses generations of men would be made to suffer and die. These excuses would reappear in the slogans of [V.I.] Lenin and [Leon] Trotsky [Communist revolutionaries], of [Adolf] Hitler and [Benito] Mussolini, of Mao Tse-tung and Ho Chi Minh, of [Fidel] Castro and [Che] Guevara, of [1970's terrorist leader Donald] De Freeze and [Yasir] Arafat.

Thus, in France in 1793–94, terror was justified not alone as a means of the survival of the French people threatened by its enemies, but also as a path to the people's welfare and virtue. In November 1793, Jean Nicolas Billaud-Varenne, the secretary of the Jacobin Club, elucidated the principles of a complete revolutionary centralization of state power to be based on the smiting ax, so that the French government could be "purified" instead of remaining "a volcano of villainy." On December 4 these postulates were formally incorporated into a law of terror.

Finally and authoritatively, Robespierre himself invoked the good of the people as the paramount reason for terror. In his speech of December 25, 1793, on "the Principles of the Revolutionary Government," the advocate from Arras intoned that the theory of this government was as new as the very revolution that gave it birth—it could be found in no books but only in the life and strife of that specific era. Robespierre explained the difference between two regimes as he saw them—the revolutionary and the constitutional. The former regime had as its task the creation of a republic; the latter, the safeguard of that republic. Robespierre viewed the world of politics quite narrowly: to him there were only two positive kinds of governments. He elucidated these two regimes: A revolution meant war by the legions of freedom against their adversaries. A constitution came after the triumph of the revolution—it was the regime of a victorious and peaceful freedom. This specific time in France was one of war. Therefore the nation's revolutionary government must defend good citizens with all possible force, implacably dealing out death to the enemies of the people.

These concepts were enough, Robespierre declaimed, to make clear the origin and nature of revolutionary laws. But the opponents of these concepts and these laws, the captious persons who called these laws tyrannical, were either stupid individuals or vice-ridden sophists. Robespierre asked: "If the revolutionary government must be more energetic in its actions and freer in its steps, does this mean that it is less just and less lawful?" He answered: "No! For it bases itself on the holiest of all laws—the good of the people; and on the most inalienable of all rights—necessity."

This argument served as an all-important part of almost every public statement by Robespierre, always ending in his call to improve yet further the work of the Revolutionary Tribunal and to bring to the guillotine blade yet another rollcall of persons, yet more categories of men and women.

Through all this, Robespierre claimed to be the truest of all the disciples of Rousseau. He reminded his listeners that Rousseau had described man as good by nature but corrupted by civilization. This idea was twisted by Robespierre into his burning conviction that man could be saved from himself, from his meanness and criminality, by the guillotine. Robespierre would help man get rid of the evil not recognized by man himself: he would restore man's pristine purity by the death penalty. By executing them en masse, this provincial lawyer would be doing his victims the valiant favor of restoring virtue to them and to society. Their execution would be less of a punishment, more of a gift—the gift of the original, inborn sinlessness returned to them as their heads rolled off the bloody block. This Republic of Virtue via Blood, ushered in by Robespierre, would surely be blessed by the Supreme Being, by Robespierre's own version of the Supreme Being, the new revolutionary deity whose worship Robespierre decreed as a new state religion, in whose honor he arranged his peculiar pageants of worship.

Robespierre Kills Thousands for His Ideological Goals

Because of this singular fanaticism, he has been called by some a mistaken idealist. In sober reality he was mistaken, but he was not an idealist. To apply this noun to him is an insult to idealism. Robespierre was a sick, demented man who caused wholesale deaths while emitting high-sounding but vapid phrases. His was not an ideology; it was a phraseology.

And yet, at first, many Frenchmen and Frenchwomen took his oratory for an ideology as well as for a viable revolutionary religion. Many willingly, even enthusiastically, followed him. As an illness often overcomes an individual by degrees, so the Grand Terror, charged up and maintained by this extraordinary zealot, grew in phases so insidious that even decent persons sometimes failed to notice they were being drawn in as his followers; too late did these followers realize that soon they were to join his victims on the tragic scaffold. Their hysterical applause for the tyrant was replaced by sheer fright when, alas, nothing was left for them to do but mount the steps and submit to the blade.

Joseph Stalin's Rule by Terror

Walter Laqueur

In 1879 the man known to history as Joseph Stalin was born in Georgia, then a poor border region in the Russian Empire, now an independent country. Josef Dzhugashvili—his birth name—was an intelligent pupil who was given a scholarship to study to become an Orthodox priest at a seminary in the Georgian capital of Tiflis. During his time there, he joined the illegal Social Democratic Party, which was dedicated to Communist revolution in Russia. It was during this time that he become known as Stalin, or "man of steel."

Stalin rose rapidly through the ranks of the party to become a member of the Central Committee, the supreme policy making council of the party. He gravitated to the Social Democratic Party's radical wing, the Bolsheviks. His faction seized power in the October Revolution of 1917. Stalin played an important part in the civil war that followed, and then outmaneuvered rivals for power and by 1930 he had achieved virtually absolute rule in Russia.

Stalin's rule was marked by show trials, purges, mass starvation of peasants, and terror. Always suspicious by nature, he became more isolated as he grew older, and more paranoid toward potential rivals. His paranoia led him to order the execution of many former allies, including Leon Trotsky, as well as thousands of ordinary Russians.

Walter Laqueur, *Stalin: The Glasnost Revelations*. London: Unwin Hyman, 1990. Copyright © 1990 by Walter Laqueur. All rights reserved. Reproduced by permission of The Gale Group.

In the following excerpt, Walter Laqueur traces Stalin's rise to power. He also explains the paradoxical relationship between Stalin and his subjects, who both feared his rule and trusted the dictator to do what was best for Russia. Despite his brutality, many Soviet citizens truly grieved Stalin's death in 1953.

Walter Laqueur holds the Henry A. Kissinger Chair in National Security Policy at the Center for Strategic and International Studies, a think tank in Washington, D.C. He is the author of numerous books on history and terrorism, including *The New Terrorism: Fanaticism and the Arms of Mass Destruction* and *A History of Terrorism*.

🐝 🐝 🐝

The essential facts about Stalin's youth and early career are relatively few, and they have been known to his biographers for a long time. While Stalin was alive, he was not interested in permitting more than a minimum amount of detail in the public realm; when he died and a freer investigation became possible, it was too late to uncover any major new details. Perhaps there was nothing to discover.

Stalin was born Josef Dzhugashvili on December 20, 1879, in Gori, a little town in the Caucasus not far from [the Georgian city of] Tiflis. His father was a hard-drinking shoemaker who died when his son was eleven years of age. Josef ("Soso") was brought up by his mother, a washerwoman. He went to the local church school, and because he was a good pupil, he won a scholarship to the Tiflis Theological Seminary. At the age of eighteen he joined a clandestine [secret] local Social Democratic party. This led to his expulsion from the seminary in 1899. One year later, following a police search of his room, he went underground. A year later, his first articles appeared in the illegal press, and he became a member of the local party executive. His party nickname was "Koba," but he also used several other aliases.

Professional Revolutionary

Between 1901 and 1917, he lived the life of a professional revolutionary, mainly in Baku, the main industrial center in the Caucasus [a mountainous region south of Russia, then part of the Russian Empire], but also, for a shorter period, in Petersburg, the capital. There were four or five arrests. On one occasion, he was exiled to Siberia, but escaped. Gradually he became known to the central leadership; in a letter to [Communist writer] Maksim Gorky, [leader of the Communist revolution Vladimir Ilich] Lenin referred to Stalin as that "splendid Georgian." A few years later, however, Lenin had forgotten Stalin's name. Stalin participated at [Communist] party congresses in Finland (1905), Stockholm (1906), and London (1907). When the Prague Conference was convened in 1912, Stalin was under arrest; in his absence, he was co-opted as a member of the [Communist Party's] Central Committee.

Rise to Power

Stalin had the reputation of a hardworking, reliable, and able party worker. Unlike many other revolutionary leaders, he was neither an outstanding orator nor a theoretician. His only major publication to appear before the revolution of 1917, "Marxism and the National Question," was written at the level of a superior seminar paper. Essentially a doer, he excelled in conspirative organizational work that included the smuggling and distribution of party literature. He also helped organize the "expropriation" of banks, that is to say, armed holdups. For this reason, in 1917, the Mensheviks [moderate Socialists] revealed that he had been excluded from the Tiflis party organization; Stalin claimed that he had never been excluded but did not deny the substance of the charge against him. He was a hard-liner who, in the various splits that occurred in Russian social democracy, always opted for the most radical wing, that is, the Bolsheviks [Communists]. He had great self-discipline, and if he nursed political ambitions, he knew well to hide them. He was a dynamic, fearless, indefatigable party workhorse, at least until his last, longest internment in 1913.

During the next four years of exile in Turukhansk, Siberia, he became curiously lethargic. He did not attempt to escape, and although other Bolshevik exiles used their years in Siberia to study, read, and write, Stalin's only passion seems to have been hunting and fishing. There were rumors that he had been enlisted as an agent by the Okhrana, the tsarist secret police, but this has never been proved. He left Siberia only after the February Revolution [the revolution in 1917 that brought the end of the Russian Empire and the beginning of democratic government] and the fall of the tsarist regime.

Personal Life
Stalin had no close friends; he was sullen, rude, and had other (unspecified) character traits that made many party comrades shun his company. In 1903, he married a girl, Ekaterina (Keke) Svanidze, from a neighboring Georgian village, who died four years later. There was one child from this marriage, Yasha, who was taken prisoner of war in 1941 and died in a German camp. Stalin is said to have fathered another child in his Siberian exile; if so, he showed no interest in his offspring at the time or in later years. But then, Stalin was never a family man; his mother went on to live for many years after the Revolution, yet Stalin saw her only once. Perhaps he felt embarrassed by the presence of the illiterate wash-

erwoman; perhaps he did not care one way or another.

The man who arrived in Petrograd in 1917 and who had adopted the name Stalin a number of years earlier (between 1910 and 1912) was thirty-eight years of age—not a youngster by the standard of those days but a mature revolutionary. (Lenin, his elder by nine years, was known as *Starik*, the "old man.")

Stalin was small in stature but of powerful physique; he had a pockmarked face, and his famous mustache seems to have been in place since the year 1900. He had a quick intelligence and a phenomenal memory but little education and few interests outside Russian working-class politics. His command of the Russian language was perfect, but he spoke with a strong Georgian accent. As a member of the "Russian bureau" of the Bolsheviks, he was a high-ranking official; yet, in 1917, he was probably the least-known leader of comparable rank both inside the party and, *a fortiori* [even more so], outside it.

He played no leading role in the year of the two revolutions. In accounts at the time of the Revolution, he is seldom, if ever, mentioned, except as a member of the Executive Committee of the party. One such report characterized him as creating the impression of a "gray blur, looming up now and then dimly and not leaving any trace." In later years, after most of his erstwhile comrades had died or had been executed, Stalin rewrote Soviet history to include his participation, together with Lenin, in planning and carrying out the Revolution. Nothing could be further from the truth; his role in 1917 was exceedingly modest. True, he was not a gray blur or a mediocrity or the "creature of the party bureaucracy" claimed by [Communist leader Leon] Trotsky in later years. His career was not made as a people's tribune; his influence was based on patient organizational work carried out in small meetings in back rooms, far from street crowds and large assemblies. Yet his work was recognized, and when the first list of fifteen ministers ("people's commissars") was published after the uprising, Stalin's name was among them—the people's commissar for nationalities.

The Stalin Legend

There are interesting divergences between the Stalin legend and the real facts, even prior to 1917. He came from modest beginnings in a border area of the Russian Empire, which had to be played down because it was not befitting the image of the great leader, just as the terrorist incidents had to be suppressed. These aspects of his background were not compatible with the image of a wise statesman, the father of his people. He thought of himself as a Russian, and he was to be described as such. But how significant is it, in the final analysis, that Stalin, at the age of twenty-three in Batum [a city and port in Russia], or a few years later in Baku [capital city of Azerbaijan, then a region in Russia], was not yet a leader of world stature and renown, but instead played second fiddle to [Georgian Communist leader Stepan] Shaumyan and others, and that the stage of his activities was a little sideshow? He had not yet arrived at the center of the Russian political scene, and for this reason, if for no other, after 1930, the rewriting of history about his early years is not of great importance.

All this begins to change with the October Revolution [the revolution in 1917 when the Communists seized power in Russia], when the biography of Josef Stalin gradually turns into the history of the Soviet Union. During the civil war he played a role of some importance, above all in the defense of [the Russian city of] Tsaritsyn; later, Stalingrad; later yet, Volgograd. He was also sent on special missions to other parts of the front. In the year 1919, he was appointed a member of the Politburo, the highest executive body of the party.

Three years later, Stalin became secretary-general of the party. The office of the secretariat, founded in 1919, had been of no great consequence before, but Stalin made it into the seat of real power. When, shortly before his death [in 1924], Lenin tried to remove Stalin, it was too late; Lenin's famous "Testament" was ignored by the party. Trotsky, the leader next in stature to Lenin, was a brilliant speaker and writer but an incompetent tactician. Trotsky maneuvered himself into a position that effectively debarred him from the struggle for the succession. From 1923, the country was ruled by a triumvirate consisting of Stalin, [Grigory Yeveseyevich] Zinoviev, and [Lev Barisovich] Kamenev.

Purges and Mass Trials

In 1925, Stalin made a turn to the right, got rid of his two companions, and established a coalition with such moderate leaders as [Nikolai] Bukharin, [Alexei] Rykov, and [Mikhail] Tomsky, which lasted until 1928, when the collectivization of agriculture and the forced industrialization of the Five-Year Plans came about. By that time Stalin had established his own apparatus within, the party, and those who were not his faithful followers were systematically replaced. By 1930, his rule was absolute, and within another few years, the Stalinist system had been established—euphemistically labeled "cult of the individual," rule by propaganda and terror.

The purges and mass trials at first seemed rational inasmuch as the main victims were former enemies and rivals, or at least potential foes. But gradually they became quite unpredictable, and they began to affect Stalin's blind, unquestioning followers.

During the 1930s, Stalin the boss (*khoziain*) became a great statesman, a great ideologist—for the time being, merely continuing Lenin's work, whose most faithful pupil he was—and a great economist. With the German invasion in June 1941, Stalin also became a supreme military leader. No leader in modern history, with the possible exception of Adolf Hitler, had concentrated so much power in his hands. But Hitler led his country to defeat, whereas the Soviet Union emerged triumphant from the war. Thus, in 1945, Stalin was at the height of his power; his prestige was equally great at home and abroad. Under his leadership, the Soviet Union had emerged as the strongest power in Europe by far and as a world power equal to the United States.

Stalin Mourned at His Death

That Stalin's last years were, in most respects, anticlimactic appears most clearly only after his death in 1953. Those who had hoped for more freedom and greater prosperity inside the Soviet Union were disappointed; the propaganda and terror machine relentlessly continued its work, the arrests and the executions continued, and the Soviet Union remained an empire of fear. Stalin's intellectual preoccupations and ambitions became even more splenetic [bad tempered]; he even wrote pseudoscientific essays on linguistics. The economic rebuilding of the ravaged country was initiated and made some progress, but less so than in many other countries. Soviet power was consolidated in the Eastern European countries, which had been occupied in the last phase of the war. But it was imposed in such a way as to plant the seeds of opposition and conflict—first with Yugoslavia, later with other Communist countries.

When Stalin died in 1953, he was mourned by many of his subjects; whether there was a genuine feeling of bereavement or whether they were fearful about the future, we do not know. Stalin had systematically inculcated the belief that only he was farsighted enough to lead the country, that without him the Soviet people would be lost, an easy prey to the country's many enemies.

However, a good number of Stalin's subjects genuinely admired him and sincerely thought his form of rule the most adequate for their country. Why they should have thought so, why they should have genuinely missed him, is one of the central questions this study wishes to address. . . .

Stalin and his system were apparently genuinely popular; he was an excellent father figure for tens of millions of his subjects, strict but fair and wise. It does not explain, however, why many of his subjects continued to believe, at least to some extent, in Stalin and Stalinism even after his death, when the crimes and failures of the system had already become common knowledge. This can be explained only against the background of the lack of a democratic tradition in Russia, a country ruled for centuries by autocrats, unfettered by constitutional restraints. True, some of the rulers had been more autocratic than others, but the people by and large had accepted them not just dutifully as a necessary evil but with genuine respect and even love (as if they were sent by God), not to be resisted, however foolishly or cruelly they behaved.

Adolf Hitler's Rise to Power in Germany

Sebastian Haffner

Adolf Hitler, one of the most reviled dictators in history, was for the first thirty years of his life an obscure failure in Germany and post–World War I Vienna. Then, beginning in 1919, he rose from leader of a small, right-wing reactionary political party to absolute ruler of Germany's Third Reich and Europe's Axis powers. His Nazi regime plunged Europe into World War II and his genocidal policies caused the death of millions before his defeat and death in 1945.

German author and journalist Sebastian Haffner gives a concise sketch of Hitler's life in the following selection. According to Haffner, Hitler had no other life but politics, lacking such basic elements of life as friends, a spouse, children, and trade skills. The important features of Hitler's life are all political: his hatred of communism, his hatred of the Jews, and his will to restore German power at the cost of destroying a continent.

🐝 🐝 🐝

Sebastian Haffner, "Life," *The Meaning of Hitler*, translated by Ewald Osers. New York: Macmillan Publishing Co., Inc., 1979. Copyright © 1979 by Ewald Osers. All rights reserved. Reproduced by permission of The Gale Group.

Adolf Hitler's father made a success of life. The illegitimate son of a servant girl, he rose to become a state official of administrative rank and died honoured and respected.

His son began by making a mess of his life. He did not finish school, failed his entrance examination at the Vienna Academy of Arts, and spent the time from his eighteenth to his twenty-fifth year in Vienna [the capital of Austria] and then in [the southern German city of] Munich, doing nothing and aspiring to nothing. His orphan's pension and the occasional lucky sale of a painting kept the young Bohemian [a person who lives an unconventional lifestyle] afloat. At the outbreak of war in 1914 he volunteered for the Bavarian Army. There followed four years of front-line service, during which courage earned him both classes of the Iron Cross [a medal awarded by the German army] but lack of leadership qualities prevented him from rising above the rank of corporal. After the end of the war, which he witnessed as a gas casualty in a German military hospital, he remained a 'barracks dweller' for a further year. He still had no plans or prospects of a job. He was then thirty.

Failure Followed by Success

At that age, in the autumn of 1919, he joined a small radical Right-wing party, in which he soon played a leading role, and that was the beginning of a political career which eventually made him an historic figure.

Hitler lived from 20 April 1889 until 30 April 1945, i.e. almost exactly fifty-six years. The difference between his first thirty and the following twenty-six years seems to be inexplicable. For thirty years he was an obscure failure; then almost overnight a local celebrity and eventually the man around whom the whole of world policy revolved. How does that go together?

Although that difference has provoked numerous explanations it is in fact more apparent than real, not merely because Hitler's political career continued to be disjointed during its first ten years, and Hitler the politician turned out in the final analysis to be a failure, albeit on a supreme scale, but mainly because Hitler's personal life remained poor and stunted even during the second, public, period of his life. By contrast, closer inspection of his inner political life during the first, outwardly uneventful, decades of his life reveals many unusual features—features which foreshadowed much that followed. . . .

An Empty Life

His life lacked—'before' *and* 'after'—everything that normally lends weight, warmth and dignity to a human life: education, occupation, love and friendship, marriage, parenthood. Apart from politics and political passion, his was an empty life and hence one which, though certainly not happy, was strangely lightweight, and lightly discarded. A continuous readiness for suicide accompanied Hitler throughout his political career. And at its end, almost as a matter of course, stood a real suicide.

Hitler's celibacy and childlessness are well known. Love played an unusually slight part in his life. There were a few women, but he treated them as unimportant and did not make them happy. Eva Braun attempted suicide twice because she felt hurt and neglected ('He only needs me for certain purposes'); her predecessor, Hitler's niece Geli Raubal, actually did commit suicide—probably for the same reasons. Hitler was on an election tour and had not taken her along; her action compelled him, for once—the only time—to interrupt something that was more important to him, for her sake. Hitler mourned her and replaced her. This melancholy story is what comes closest to a great love in Hitler's life.

Hitler had no friends. He enjoyed sitting for hours on end with subordinate staff—drivers, bodyguards, secretaries—but he alone did all the talking. In this 'servants' quarters atmosphere' he unwound. Real friendship he avoided all his life. His relationships with men such as [Air Force chief Hermann] Goering, [propaganda minister Joseph] Goebbels or [secret police chief Heinrich] Himmler always remained cool and remote. [Early Nazi leader Ernst] Röhm, the only one of his paladins with whom he was on familiar terms from early days, he had shot, principally, no doubt, because he had become politically inconvenient. However, the old intimacy certainly proved no obstacle to his removal. If one reflects on Hitler's general shyness one is almost led to suspect that Röhm's superannuated claim to friendship was, if anything, an additional reason for getting rid of him.

Hitler's Lack of Education

There remain education and occupation. Hitler never enjoyed any systematic education; just a few years of *Realschule* (a lesser type of school), with poor reports. True, during his years of loafing he read a lot but—on his own admission—absorbed only what he thought he already knew. In the political sphere Hitler had the knowledge of a dedicated reader of newspapers. His only real learning was of military affairs and military technology. Here the practical experience of the front-line soldier enabled him critically to absorb what he read. Strange though it may sound, his front-line experience was probably his only education. For the rest, he remained the typical half-educated man all his life—one who always knew better and tossed about picked-up pieces of half-knowledge and wrong knowledge, preferably before an audience whom he could impress by doing so because it knew nothing at all. His table talk at his headquarters testifies to his educational gaps in an embarrassing manner.

Hitler never had nor sought an occupation; on the contrary, he positively avoided one. His shyness of occupation is as striking a trait as his shyness of marriage or intimacy. Nor could one call him a professional politician. Politics was his life but never his profession. During his early political career he variously gave his occupation as painter, writer, merchant and propaganda speaker; later he was quite simply the Führer [leader], not answerable to anyone—at first only the Führer of the Party but ultimately *Der Führer* altogether. The first political office he ever held was that of Reich Chancellor; viewed from a professional point of view he was a strange chancellor: he left the capital whenever he chose, read or did not read documents as and when he pleased, held Cabinet meetings only irregularly and after 1938 not at all. His political mode of working was never that of the top public servant but that of an unfettered independent artist waiting for inspiration, seemingly idle for days and weeks on end, and then, when the spirit moved him, throwing himself into a sudden frenzy of activity. Only in the last four years of his life did Hitler, for the first time, practise a regular activity—as military Commander-in-Chief. Then, of course, he could not play truant from the twice-daily staff conferences. And then his inspiration increasingly failed him. . . .

Failure to Mature

He lacks something else that needs mentioning briefly before we come to what is really worth considering in Hitler's life. There is no development, no maturing in Hitler's character and personality. His character was fixed at an early age—perhaps a better word would be arrested—and remains astonishingly consistent; nothing was added to it. It was not an attractive character. All soft, lovable, reconciling traits are missing unless one regards his shyness, which sometimes seems like bashfulness, as a reconciling feature. His positive characteristics—resolution, boldness, courage, perseverance—lie all on the 'hard' side. The negative ones even more so: ruthlessness, vindictiveness, faithlessness and cruelty. Added to these, moreover, from the very start, was a total lack of capacity for self-criticism. Hitler was all his life exceedingly full of himself and from his earliest to his last days tended to self-conceit. Stalin and Mao used the cult of their personality coolly as a political instrument, without letting it turn their heads. With the Hitler cult, Hitler was not only its object but also the earliest, most persistent and most passionate devotee.

Hitler's Political Life

Enough said about the person and the unprofitable personal biography of Hitler. Let us now look at what is worth looking at, his political biography which, in contrast to his personal one, is not short of development or intensification. It begins long before his first public appearance and reveals seven stages or leaps:

1. His early concentration on politics as a substitute for life.
2. His first (still private) political action—the emigration from Austria to Germany.
3. His decision to become a politician.
4. His discovery of his hypnotic abilities as a mass-audience orator.
5. His decision to become *Der Führer*.
6. His decision to adapt his political timetable to his personal expectation of life (this is simultaneously his decision to wage war).
7. His decision to commit suicide.

The last two decisions differ from the preceding ones in that they are solitary decisions. With all the others the subjective and objective sides are inseparable. They may be Hitler's decisions, but in Hitler or through Hitler the spirit of the age or the mood of the day each time acts like a gust of wind filling a sail.

Nationalism and Socialism

Even the emerging passionate political interest of the eighteen- or nineteen-year-old, who had suffered the shipwreck of his artistic ambition but carried ambition as such into his new sphere of interest, was in tune with or indeed sprang from the mood of the day. Europe before the first war was far more political than today. It was a Europe of great imperialist powers—all in permanent rivalry, all jockeying for position, all in permanent readiness for war. That was exciting to everybody. It also was a Europe of class conflicts and of the promised or feared Red [Communist] Revolution. That too was exciting. In one way or another, politics was the subject at any table of regulars at a middle-class café and in any proletarian tavern. The private lives, not only of the workers but also of the middle classes, were much narrower and poorer than they are today. But in the evening, as a compensation, everyone was, with his country, a Lion or an Eagle, or, with his class, the banner-bearer of a great future. Hitler, who had nothing else to do, was that all day long. Politics was then a substitute for living—for almost everyone to a certain extent, but for the young Hitler wholly and exclusively.

Anti-Semitism Is Hitler's Primary Ideology

Nationalism and socialism were powerful mass-mobilizing slogans. Imagine the explosive power if one succeeded in somehow uniting them! It is possible, though not certain, that this idea occurred even to the young Hitler. He wrote subsequently that even at the age of twenty, in Vienna about 1910, he had laid 'the granite foundations' of his political ideology—but whether that ideology is justified in calling itself National Socialism is open to argument. The real Hitlerian bedrock, his primal and lowest layer, which took shape during his Vienna period, is certainly not a fusion of nationalism and socialism but a fusion of nationalism and anti-semitism. Anti-semitism was the primary element, and this Hitler carried with him from the start, like a congenital hump. But his nationalism too, a very special Greater-German nationalism, undoubtedly dates back to his time in Vienna. His socialism, however, is most probably a later addition.

Hitler's anti-semitism is an East European plant. In Western Europe and also in Germany anti-semitism was on the wane about the turn of the century; assimilation and integration of the Jews was desired and was in full swing. But in Eastern and South Eastern Europe, where the numerous Jews were living, voluntarily or involuntarily, as a separate nation within the nation, anti-semitism was (and is?) endemic and murderous, directed not towards assimilation or integration but towards liquidation and extermination. And this murderous East European anti-semitism, which allowed the Jews no escape, reached as far as Vienna in whose third district, according to Metternich's famous dictum, the Balkans begin. There the youthful Hitler picked it up. How, we do not know. There is no record of any disagreeable personal experience, and he himself never claimed anything of the kind. According to his account in *Mein Kampf* the observation that Jews were different people was enough for the conclusion, 'Because they are different they have to be removed.'

Mao Zedong and the Cultural Revolution

Jonathan Spence

Born in 1893, Mao Zedong's early years were in a China ruled by an emperor. He rose from a peasant background to become chairman of the Chinese Communist Party and thus absolute ruler of China. He struggled for more than two decades against warlords, the Nationalist Chinese of Chiang Kai-shek, and Japanese invaders to achieve his goal of a Communist revolution in China.

After the Communists seized complete power in 1949, Mao turned all his energies to making his country competitive with the West and his Soviet Communist rivals. To speed up this process, he ordered that all peasant farmers be "collectivized" in large communes. He also started large industrialization projects such as giant dams. These attempts at rapid modernization disrupted Chinese agriculture and industry; the result was widespread famine in which up to 30 million people died.

Unable to accept responsibility for the failure of his policies, Mao blamed Chinese society itself. Starting in the mid-1960s, he instituted the Cultural Revolution, an attempt to make over Chinese society through radical upheaval. The first targets of his repression were political

Jonathan Spence, *Mao Zedong*. New York: Viking Penguin, 1999. Copyright © 1999 by Viking Penguin. Reproduced by permission of Penguin Books, Ltd.

rivals, intellectuals, and writers. He then encouraged
youths and students to revolt against teachers, shop owners, and factory managers. Every trace of both traditional
Chinese society and Western influence was to be rooted
out. Those who objected were jailed, executed, or even
beaten to death by mobs. This decade of turmoil and destruction came to an end as Mao's health declined. Mao
was able to hold on to rule until his death in 1976.

The following selection on the Cultural Revolution is
excerpted from a biography of Mao by eminent China
scholar Jonathan Spence.

M ao seems to have encouraged his immediate family to lead as ordinary a life as possible and not to take
an active part in politics, but he was not so protective of
his brothers' families. Mao Yuanxin, for example, the
son of Mao's younger brother Mao Zemin (executed in
Xinjiang in 1943) was enrolled in the Harbin Institute
of Military Engineering in 1964, and Mao used him as
a foil for many of his own ideas. Their exchanges were
later published. From Mao's questions to his nephew,
we can see that he was feeling out a field for himself, in
which the next round of the battle could be fought to
his advantage. The fact that there was a definite enemy—the forces of "bourgeois revisionism" inside
China determined to undermine the revolution—was
already firming up in Mao's mind. These enemies
might be found anywhere: in rural production brigades
and urban factories, in Party committees and public security departments, and in the ministry of culture and
the film industry. They were even among the students
in Mao Yuanxin's own institute, listening secretly to
overseas radio broadcasts and filling their diaries with

subversive material. "They" were also behind the role system of lecturing and the pointless examinations that schools used to judge a person's performance.

Now, at the age of seventy, Mao was clearly obsessed with revolutionary continuity and his belief that the young people like Yuanxin would have to bear the standard forward. Five elements were essential in this succession, Mao told his nephew: one must be a genuine Marxist-Leninist; one must be willing to serve the masses wholeheartedly; one must work with the majority and accept their criticisms, even if the criticisms seemed misplaced at the time; one must be a model of obedient discipline under the strictures of democratic centralism; and one must be modest about oneself, always ready to indulge in self-criticism. Looking at his nephew, Mao added the harsh judgment: "You grew up eating honey, and thus far you have never known suffering. In future, if you do not become a rightist, but rather a centrist, I shall be satisfied. You have never suffered, how can you be a leftist?"

With these last words, Mao had posed a question that was to obsess him and many of China's youth into the early years of the Cultural Revolution. His answer was to be based on the idea that waning leftist revolutionary activism could be regenerated by identifying the enemies correctly, and then using all one's ingenuity in rooting them out and destroying them. Mao had stated in the past that it was necessary to "set fires" every few years to keep the revolution alive. But doing that could also frighten people: "It's certainly not easy to set a fire to burn oneself. I've heard that around this area there were some people who had second thoughts and didn't set a big fire." Mao came to see his mission as partly to set the fire, but also to teach the young to do it for themselves.

In this strangely apocalyptic mission, Mao found a

loose association of allies. One was the defense minister, Lin Biao, who was willing to lead the People's Liberation Army forward into revolution, via the "little red book" of Mao's thought, which Lin commissioned in 1964 and ordered every soldier to read. A year later Lin Biao ordered the abolition of insignia, Soviet-style uniforms, and other signs of officer status throughout the army, re-creating—at least in Mao's mind—an image of the simpler guerrilla aura of military life with which Mao had so long been associated. A second group of allies consisted of certain intellectuals and cadres, many of them based in Shanghai, who had a strongly leftist orientation and were genuinely dismayed by what they saw as the backward-looking direction of industrial and rural policy. A third was centered on Mao's wife, Jiang Qing, who for twenty years after their marriage in Yan'an had not been active in politics. But in 1956, after returning from her medical trip to the Soviet Union, she began to take a lively interest in the current state of film and theater in China. Gradually she formed a nucleus of fellow believers who sought to reinstill revolutionary attitudes into the cultural world and to root out those revisionist elements that—she agreed with Mao—were lurking everywhere. A fourth ally was Kang Sheng, a revolutionary Shanghai labor organizer and spymaster in the 1920s, later trained in police techniques in the Soviet Union. He had introduced Mao to Jiang Qing in Yan'an, and later became head of the Central Committee's security apparatus and of the Central Party School. Kang Sheng had been a pioneer in orchestrating a literary inquisition to prove that rightists were "using novels to promote anti-Party activities."

It was natural for these disparate forces to gradually coalesce, to find novelists, dramatists, historians, and philosophers on whom to pile their criticisms, and to use Shanghai as a base for mass campaigns that could also be coordinated with the army's various cultural departments. Once the apparatus of leftist criticism was in place in the cultural sphere, it could easily be switched to tackle problems of education in schools and universities, the municipal Party committees that were technically in charge of those cultural realms or educational systems, and the individual Party leaders to whom those committees reported. If galvanized from the center, a remarkable force might be generated.

Mao's Hostility Toward Intellectuals

By late 1965 this was exactly what began to happen. Mao was frustrated with the laggardly implementation of revolutionary policies, and genuinely suspicious of his own bureaucracy. He had grown to distrust the head of state, Liu Shaoqi, and to be skeptical about Liu's ability to guide the revolution after Mao. Mao also had grown more hostile to intellectuals as the years went by—perhaps because he knew he would never really be one, not even at the level of his own secretaries, whom he would commission to go to the libraries to track down classical sources for him and help with historical references. Mao knew, too, that scholars of the old school like Deng Tuo, the man he had summarily ousted from the *People's Daily*, had their own erudite circles of friends with whom they pursued leisurely hours of classical connoisseurship, which was scarcely different from the lives they might have enjoyed under the old society. They wrote elegant and amusing essays, which were printed in various literary newspapers, that used allegory and analogy to tease the kind of "commandism" that had been so present in the Great Leap,[1] and indeed in the Communist leadership as a whole. It was surely of such

1. the Great Leap Forward, Mao's failed attempt to collectivize agriculture in the 1950s

men that Mao was thinking when he wrote: "All wisdom comes from the masses. I've always said that intellectuals are the most lacking in intellect. The intellectuals cock their tails in the air, and they think, 'If I don't rank number one in all the world, then I'm at least number two.'"

Mao did not precisely orchestrate the coming of the Cultural Revolution, but he established an environment that made it possible and helped to set many of the people and issues in place. In November 1965 a new round of polemics appeared in a Shanghai journal, attacking the historian Wu Han, who was the direct subordinate of the powerful Party boss Peng Zhen, controller of a five-man group that was the arbiter of the Beijing cultural realm. Peng Zhen was unprepared to handle the onslaught, though publication of the article in Beijing was blocked by his staff. Seizing on the chance disruption as a good trigger for action, Mao moved swiftly to remove the head of the Central Committee's general office, which controlled the flow of crucial information for senior Party leaders. It must have been an added inducement to Mao that this man was Yang Shangkun, who had ordered the bugging devices planted in Mao's personal train and in the guest houses where he stayed. In Yang's place, Mao appointed the head of the central Beijing garrison, whom he knew to be fiercely loyal.

At the same time, Lin Biao began to replace key personnel at the top of the military, including the current army chief of staff and former minister of security Luo Ruiqing. In March 1966, after months of relentless questioning about his political loyalties and his attitudes toward political indoctrination in the army ranks, as well as a major series of "struggle sessions" with his inquisitors, Luo tried to commit suicide by jumping from a building. Mao's wife, Jiang Qing, joined the fray by briefing army commanders on the bourgeois decadence and corruption in the arts, which led to the publication of a joint "army forum on literature and art work." Mao had already, in a meeting with his secretaries, shared with them his conviction that the works of the historian Wu Han were intended to be defenses of Peng Dehuai in his earlier struggle at Lushan, and he proceeded to deepen the attacks on the Beijing party and cultural establishment. Lin Biao sharpened tension by warning that the "right" was planning a coup against Mao. Security was tightened in the Zhongnanhai residential area. Two men knew, as well as any in China, what all this must portend. They were Deng Tuo, the former editor of *People's Daily*, and Tian Jiaying, Mao's confidential secretary for eighteen years, who had reported negatively on the peasants' feelings about communes. In the last weeks of May, both men committed suicide.

Red Guards Form

Much of this struggle had taken place in secret, or at least in the well-insulated world of the Party hierarchy. But in late May, some Beijing University teachers put up wall posters denouncing the rightists, or "capitalist-roaders," in their campuses and in the cultural bureaucracy; Mao endorsed the posters, and students began to follow suit, with attacks against their own teachers. *People's Daily* editorialized in favor of the dissidents, and the movement spread to other cities in China, and from colleges to high schools. Groups of students began to wear paramilitary uniforms with red armbands and to declare themselves Red Guards and defenders of Chairman Mao. Mao himself, who had been watching these events from the security of a guest house in the celebrated beauty spot of Hangzhou, traveled in July to Wuhan and took a leisurely swim down the Yangtze, which was rapturously publicized across the nation as proof of the chairman's energy and fitness.

Returning to Beijing, Mao reconstituted the Politburo Standing Committee, to remove or demote those he had identified as his enemies. As for himself, Mao wrote in a brief editorial comment that appeared in *People's Daily:* "My wish is to join all the comrades of our party to learn from the masses, to continue to be a schoolboy." In August, with the oracular pronouncement that "to rebel is justified," and that it was good "to bombard the headquarters," Mao donned military uniform and from the top of Tiananmen reviewed hundreds of thousands of chanting students, accepting from them a Red Guard armband as evidence of his support. By September, several of the rallies were attended by a million people, who began to flock to Beijing from around China. The students from Beijing, in turn, began to travel the countryside in squads—free train travel was made available to them—to spread the word of what was now called the Cultural Revolution.

Violence of the Cultural Revolution

The violence of the Cultural Revolution was manifested at two levels. One of these was orchestrated from the political center, which was now controlled by a small group totally loyal to Mao, through what was called "The Central Case Examination Group," chaired by China's premier Zhou Enlai but directly accountable to Mao. In its heyday this group was composed of eleven Party members, including Jiang Qing, Chen Boda, and Kang Sheng. Under this leadership group were three bureaus that were assigned their own cases and worked closely with the Beijing garrison command, the army general staff, and the Ministry of Public Security. They investigated 1,262 "principal cases" and an unknown number of "related case offenders."

The job of the three bureaus was to prove the correctness of "rightist" charges—including being Taiwan or Guomindang spies, or "Khrushchev-type persons"—and to use whatever means were necessary to achieve that goal. Torture, sleep deprivation, round-the-clock group interrogations, withholding of food, and many types of mental and physical pressure were used by the case investigators. In virtually all cases their victims were prominent or even once-revered revolutionaries. Peng Dehuai was brought back from Sichuan to face his own group of investigators. Incarcerated in high-security prisons (of which Qincheng was the most terrifyingly notorious), the victims could not write letters home or see family. Letters they wrote to Mao or Zhou Enlai requesting more compassionate treatment were filed away, unread. Only "confessions" were considered a tolerable form of writing.

These political prisoners only encountered the outside "revolutionary masses" at carefully orchestrated occasions. Red Guard groups would use printed forms to apply to "borrow" one of the victims, as long as they were "returned promptly." Red Guard units might have to pay the cost of renting a place for these confrontations, which would then be advertised in advance. Certain "struggle rallies" were postponed in case of rain, and some victims were in such demand that their appearances had to be limited to three denunciations a week. Liu Shaoqi died from these experiences, as did Peng Dehuai. Deng Xiaoping survived, perhaps because Mao only intended to intimidate him, not to destroy him altogether. This system of case investigation was spread systematically to the provinces, and by the end of the Cultural Revolution in 1976 as many as two million cadres had been investigated by these or similar means.

The second level of cultural revolutionary violence was unorchestrated, coursing down its own channels in an only vaguely designated direction, in search of rightists or "feudal remnants," "snakes and monsters," or "people in authority taking the capitalist road." An announcement from the "Beijing Number 26 Middle School Red Guards," dated August 1966, gave the kind of program that was to be followed by countless others. Every street was to have a quotation from Chairman Mao prominently displayed, and loudspeakers at every intersection and in all parks were to broadcast his thought. Every household as well as all trains and buses, bicycles and pedicabs, had to have a picture of Mao on its walls. Ticket takers on trains and buses should all declaim Mao's thought. Every bookstore had to stock Mao's quotations, and every hand in China had to hold one. No one could wear blue jeans, tight pants, "weird women's outfits," or have "slick hairdos or wear rocket shoes." No perfumes or beauty creams could be used. No one could keep pet fish, cats, or dogs, or raise fighting crickets. No shop could sell classical books. All those identified by the masses as landlords, hooligans, rightists, and capitalists had to wear a plaque identifying themselves as such whenever they went out. The minimum amount of persons in any room could be three—all other space had to be given to the state housing bureaus. Children should criticize their elders, and students their teachers. No one under thirty-five might smoke or drink. Hospital service would be simplified, and "complicated treatment must be abolished"; doctors had to write their prescriptions legibly, and not use English words. All schools and colleges were to combine study with productive labor and farmwork. As a proof of its own transformation, the "Number 26 Middle School" would change its name, effective immediately, to "The Maoism School."

Victims

The number of victims from the uncoordinated violence of the Cultural Revolution is incalculable, but there were many millions. Some of these were killed, some committed suicide. Some were crippled or scarred emotionally for life. Others were tormented for varying periods of time, for an imprecise number of "crimes," such as having known foreigners, owned foreign books or art objects, indulged in classical studies, been dictatorial teachers, or denigrated Mao or the Party through some chance remark. Children suffered for their parents' or grandparents' deeds, or sought to clear themselves of such charges by exhibiting unusual "revolutionary zeal," which might include trashing their own parents' apartments, beating up their schoolteachers, or going to border areas to "serve the people" and "learn from the masses." Many families destroyed their own art objects, burned or shredded their family photographs, diaries, and letters, all of which might be purloined by roving Red Guards. Many Red Guards units fought each other, sometimes to the death, divided along lines of local allegiance or class background, or by occupation, as in the case of some labor union members, construction workers, even prison wardens.

The tiny figure atop the rostrum at Tiananmen, waving his hand in a slow sideways motion to the chanting sea of red flags and little red books spread out before him as far as the eye could see, had only the faintest inklings of the emotions passing through the minds of the weeping faithful. It was enough that they were there, chanting and with tears in their eyes. It was enough that to them he had become, at last, the "Great Helmsman, great teacher, great leader, and the Red, Red sun in their hearts."

Pol Pot's Killing Fields

David P. Chandler

Born in 1925 to a peasant family in Cambodia, Saloth Sar, who came to be known as Pol Pot, received his basic education in a Buddhist monastery. He went to technical college and on to Paris (Cambodia was then a French colony) to study electronics in 1949. He spent more time on revolutionary activities than on his studies, however, and returned to Cambodia without a degree in 1953. After his return, he worked on a banana plantation and as a schoolteacher, all the while plotting revolution.

Eventually Pol Pot's plotting was successful. His group, the Red Khmer, better known as the Khmer Rouge, took power in Cambodia in 1975. Upon attaining power, Saloth Sar changed his name to Pol Pot, a common Cambodian name with no independent meaning. His adoption of a common name fit with his almost anonymous rule. Seldom seen or heard in public, Pol Pot and his close advisers used terror to radically transform Cambodian society while remaining virtually hidden from public view. They instituted a program of cleansing Cambodia of foreign influence. People who had been educated, especially in the West, or who lived in cities were literally marched to the countryside and forced to work on collective farms.

About two hundred thousand Cambodians were executed

David P. Chandler, *Brother Number One*. New York: Westview Press, 1992. Copyright © 1992 by Westview Press, Inc. Reproduced by permission of Westview Press, Inc., a member of Perseus Books, LLC.

in purges, but an estimated million more people died in the fields, worked to death. In Pol Pot's view, these city people were expendable. Pol Pot lost power when the Vietnamese, fellow Communists, invaded Cambodia in 1979. However, he fled to the jungles of Cambodia and continued to lead a guerrilla force until he was arrested by a former Khmer Rouge comrade in 1996. He died under arrest in 1998.

David P. Chandler is the author of six books on Cambodia. He has been visiting professor at Johns Hopkins University and a consultant to the United Nations and the U.S. Department of Defense.

❧   ❧   ❧

On April 17, 1975, Cambodia emerged from five traumatic years of invasions, bombardment, and civil war when its capital, Phnom Penh, fell to the guerrilla armies known as the Red Khmer, which had been besieging it since the beginning of the year. The city's population included over one million refugees, driven from their homes in rural areas. During the course of the civil war, half a million Cambodians were killed. People in the cities, without knowing much about the Red Khmer, presumed that peace would be better than war and that Cambodians, working together, could reconstruct their country.

Abolishing Cambodian Society
What happened next took everyone but the Red Khmer commanders by surprise. Within a week, the people of Phnom Penh, Battambang, and other cities were driven into the countryside by the Red Khmer and told to take up agricultural tasks. Thousands of evacuees, especially the very young and the very old, died over the next few weeks. Some survivors, walking toward regions where

they hoped their relatives would welcome them, were on the road for over a month. When they asked questions of the heavily armed young soldiers who accompanied them, they were told to obey the "revolutionary organization" (*angkar padevat*), which would act as their "mother and father." The evacuees were called "new people" or "April 17 people" because they had joined the revolution so late. Residents of the countryside were known as "base people" and were treated less harshly than the others.

After emptying the cities, the revolutionary organization embarked on a program of social transformation that affected every aspect of Cambodian life. Money, markets, and private property were abolished. Schools, universities, and Buddhist monasteries were closed. No publishing was allowed; the postal system was abolished; freedom of movement, exchanging information, personal adornment, and leisure activities were curtailed. Punishments for infractions were severe, and repeat offenders were imprisoned under harsh conditions or killed. Everyone was asked to perform tasks set for them by the revolutionary organization. For evacuee city dwellers, these tasks seldom had any relation to their training or skills. Instead, nearly all of them became peasants and were made to wear identical black cotton clothing. . . .

Mysterious Leader, Utopian Goals

The prime minister [elected to lead the revolutionary government], a rubber plantation worker called Pol Pot, was impossible to identify. At the moment he took power, just when he might have been expected to step into the open, he concealed himself behind a revolutionary name.

Who was he?

He revealed almost nothing about himself. When he

made a state visit to China in September 1977, Cambodia watchers identified Pol Pot as a forty-nine-year old former schoolteacher named Saloth Sar, who had been secretary of the Central Committee of the clandestine Communist party of Kampuchea (CPK) since 1963. Pol Pot had announced the existence of the CPK for the first time in a triumphal speech just before leaving for China. But very few Cambodians knew he was Saloth Sar. He admitted his former identity only after he had been overthrown in 1979.

Mystery clung to him as news of what was happening in Cambodia between 1975 and 1978—the DK [Democratic Kampuchea, the new name for Cambodia] period—filtered into the outside world. Most of the news was horrible. Refugees spoke of forced labor, starvation, random executions, and the tyrannical, anonymous "Organization."

What did Pol Pot and his colleagues have in mind?

This handful of men and women presided over the purest and most thoroughgoing Marxist-Leninist movement in an era of revolutions. No other regime tried to go so quickly or so far. No other inflicted as many casualties on the country's population.

At one level, the revolution was a courageous, doomed attempt by a group of Utopian thinkers to break free from the capitalist world system, abandon the past, and rearrange the future. Radicals in other countries interpreted events in Cambodia in this way. At another level, the revolution sprang from a colossal misreading of Cambodia's political capacities, its freedom of maneuver vis-à-vis its neighbors, and the interests of the rural poor on whose behalf the revolution was ostensibly being waged. At a third level, Pol Pot and his colleagues displayed a thirst for power and an unlimited capacity for distrust. Believing himself surrounded by enemies— a view he shared with, and may have derived from, [So-

viet dictator Joseph] Stalin—Pol Pot approved the torture and execution of almost twenty thousand enemies
(*khmang*) at the regime's interrogation facility in Phnom
Penh, known by the code name S-21. And thousands
more died in the regional purges he set in motion in
1977. Most of those put to death at S-21 were loyal
members of the party. Victims elsewhere, for the most
part, seem to have been innocent of treason. . . .

Pol Pot's Terror Had Forerunners

The mayhem that Democratic Kampuchea inflicted on
its people led the French author Jean Lacouture to coin
the word *autogenocide*—to differentiate events in Cambodia from previous pogroms, holocausts, purges, and
vendettas. Lacouture's horror, if not the word he
coined, was justified by the facts. In less than four years,
more than one million Cambodians, or one in seven,
probably died from malnutrition, overwork, and misdi-
agnosed or mistreated illness. At least 100,000, and
probably more, were executed for crimes against the
state. Tens of thousands perished in the conflict with
Vietnam, almost certainly started by the Red Khmer.
But was what happened autogenocide, without forerun-
ners elsewhere? Clear parallels, and probably inspira-
tions, can be found in China's Great Leap Forward in
the 1950s, the Soviet collectivization of Ukraine twenty
years before that, and purges in both countries of "elements" considered dangerous to revolutionary leaders.
In a sense, what happened in Cambodia, although more
intense, was standard operating procedure in countries
whose politics Pol Pot—or "Brother Number One," as
he was informally known to subordinates—admired. . . .

Who Was Pol Pot?

The man known to the world as Pol Pot started life with
the name Saloth Sar. Pol Pot was his revolutionary name.

When he announced his pseudonym in 1976, he followed precedents set by several Communist leaders, including [Russian Communist Vladimir] Lenin, [Soviet dictator Joseph] Stalin, [Yugoslav dictator Josef Broz] Tito, and [Vietnamese leader] Ho Chi Minh. Their intentions, when in the underground, were to conceal their true identities from the police and in some cases to inspire their followers ("Stalin," for example, means "steel"; "Ho Chi Minh" means "the enlightened one"). Pol Pot, however, took a new name after he had come to power, concealing his former identity from the nation he was about to govern. The name he chose, although common enough among rural Cambodians (the Khmer), had no independent meaning.

In making this bizarre, self-effacing gesture, Saloth Sar/Pol Pot was behaving true to form. Beginning in the 1950s, he preferred working in secret to living in the open. When Pol Pot came to power in 1976, it took analysts more than a year to identify him with certainty as a former schoolteacher named Saloth Sar who had been the secretary of the Cambodian Communist party since 1963. Pol Pot admitted his original name offhandedly to an interviewer in 1979, several months after he had been driven from power.

Over the years this extraordinarily reclusive figure concealed, clouded, and falsified so many details about his life that it is not surprising that there is even some confusion about his date of birth. North Korean radio announced in 1977 (before Pol Pot had been identified as Saloth Sar) that he had been born in 1925. French colonial records prepared in Cambodia in the 1950s, however, state that he was born on May 25, 1928. The second date, which leaves less time unaccounted for, seemed more plausible than the earlier one to many writers but has been contradicted by Saloth Sar's siblings in recent interviews. Pol Pot himself insisted on the earlier date in his interview with Nate Thayer in 1997. For these reasons, 1925 is now the preferred year of birth.

Saloth Sar's parents were ethnic Khmer. He was born in the village of Prek Sbauv, less than two miles west of the provincial capital of Kompong Thom, some ninety miles north of Phnom Penh. His father, Pen Saloth, was a prosperous farmer with nine hectares of rice land, several draft cattle, and a comfortable tile-roofed house. Saloth Sar's mother, Sok Nem, was widely respected in the district for her piety and good works. Sar was the eighth of nine children, two of whom were girls. Five of the nine survived into the 1990s.

Palace Connections

What set the family apart from others in the region were its connections with the Royal Palace in Phnom Penh. Saloth Sar's cousin Meak joined the royal ballet in the 1920s in the closing years of the reign of King Sisowath (r. 1904–1927). She soon became a consort of the king's eldest son, Prince Sisowath Monivong, and bore him a son, Kossarak, shortly before Monivong became king in 1927. She held the favored position of *khun preab me neang*—literally, "lady in charge of the women"—from which she controlled the women of the palace. The post was abolished after Monivong's death, but Meak continued to live near the Royal Palace and was attached to the *corps de ballet* as a senior teacher until the early 1970s.

Saloth Sar's family enjoyed other royal connections. In the late 1920s, Sar's older brother Loth Suong went to Phnom Penh to work at the palace as a clerk. Soon after, their sister Saloth Roeung (nicknamed Saroeun) joined the ballet and at some point in the 1930s became a consort of King Monivong. Suong worked in the palace as a clerk until 1975 and in the early 1940s married a dancer, Chea Samy. Saroeun, a favorite consort of the king, returned to Kompong Thom after Monivong's death in 1941 and eventually married a local policeman.

In 1934 or 1935, when Saloth Sar was nine years old, he and his older brother Chhay were sent by their parents to live with Meak and Suong in Phnom Penh. Sar probably would have preferred the relatively carefree life of Prek Sbauv to the more demanding one of being raised by busy relatives in a strange city. Informal adoptions by prosperous relatives are a traditional feature of Cambodian life and therefore should not be taken as indicating estrangement between children and their natural parents. In fact, although Sar's brother and sister-in-law have insisted that Sar got along well with his parents, he is not known to have mentioned them in conversations with other people. This silence, however, may be related to a conscious effacement of personal information rather than to animosity. There is no evidence that he had conflicts with his father of the sort that characterized the adolescent years of Stalin, Mao Zedong, and other prominent political figures. Indeed, his sister told an interviewer in 1997 that Saloth Sar had come back to Prek Sbauv for his father's funeral in the late 1950s and contributed to the cost of erecting a memorial *stupa*. In later life, Sar never mentioned his palace connections. Instead, he tended to emphasize his rural origins.

A Lovely Child

Soon after arriving in the capital, Saloth Sar spent several months as a novice at Vat Botum Vaddei, a Buddhist monastery near the palace that was favored by the royal family. At such a young age and recently separated from his parents, Sar must have been traumatized by the solemn discipline of the monastery, even though there would have been other little boys with shaven heads wearing yellow robes with him. At the Vat Botum Vaddei he learned the rudiments of Buddhism and became literate in Khmer. Sar was also forced to be obedient. Ironically, for someone who embraced atheism and xenophobia so fervently in later life, this brief period was the only time in his formal education (which lasted until 1952) in which Khmer rather than French was the language of instruction.

Loth Suong and Chea Samy, who looked after Saloth Sar in the 1940s, maintained that he was an even-tempered, polite, unremarkable child. As a primary student, Samy told the Australian journalist James Gerrand, Sar "had no difficulties with other students, no fights or quarrels." In examining his early years, I found no traumatic events and heard no anecdotes that foreshadow his years in power. People who met him as an adult found his self-effacing personality, perhaps a carryover from the image he projected as a child, hard to connect with his fearsome behavior in the 1970s. In Loth Suong's words, "The contemptible Pot [Khmer *a-Pot*] was a lovely child."

Secrecy, Purges, and Paranoia

Few survivors of the period from 1975 to 1979 refer to it nowadays as "Democratic Kampuchea." Instead, they speak of *samai a-Pot* ("the era of the contemptible Pot"), giving the period an ex post facto personal tinge. It is important to place this tendency to personalize Pot's reign alongside his own attempts to depersonalize his leadership of the party.

In 1976 and 1977, Pol Pot concentrated on retaining power, which meant changing some of the tactics that had helped him overthrow the Khmer Republic; but he also remained wary and assumed even with victory that enemies were everywhere. To emerge into the open, he thought, was to become endangered. There was no question of catching him off duty or off guard. In DK documents we overhear none of his informal arguments, table talk, or snatches of conversation. Minutes of standing committee meetings, so helpful for 1975 and 1976, are not available later on. After September 1976, Pol Pot and his colleagues became increasingly fearful of plots being mounted against them. Their response was to become even more remote.

The picture of the man that emerges from this period, however, is consistent with those from earlier times. As before, Pol Pot excelled in dealing with small groups, but colleagues of inferior rank now encountered him more rarely. With the Communist victory, "Brother Pol" had become prime minister. For all the talk of collectivism in Cambodia, this made him "Brother Number One." From a Communist standpoint, victory proved his correctness; from a Buddhist one, his new status demonstrated the meritoriousness of his achievements. From either perspective, he rose in prestige and became more difficult to reach.

Secrecy remained attractive to Pol Pot. It was also seen as an essential ingredient of party life. Nuon Chea expressed this view to a Danish Marxist-Leninist delegation that visited Phnom Penh in 1978. Chea's frankness can be traced to the fact that he considered his remarks confidential and never expected them to be published. "Secret work," he said, "is fundamental in all that we do. For example, the elections of comrades to leading work are secret. The places where our leaders live are secret. . . . As long as there is class struggle or imperialism, secret work will remain fundamental. Only through secrecy can we be masters of the situation and win victory over the enemy who cannot find out who is who."

In 1976–1977 Pol Pot concentrated on the "Four Year Plan to Build Socialism in All Fields" and the purging of "enemies," which was carried out in large

part at the party's interrogation center S-21 in the Phnom Penh suburb of Tuol Sleng. These programs fit
with his priorities of "building and defending" the
country. To build the country it was essential to take
charge of its economic activities; to defend it, it was essential to eliminate enemies of the state. Pol Pot later
blamed the uneven results of his all-embracing, radical
Four Year Plan on "enemies" just as Stalin and Mao Zedong had done when their grandiose economic plans
ran into trouble. The speed with which the Cambodian
plan was set in motion, moreover, was traced to the ur-
gency of defeating the "enemies" before they could
sabotage it. In Pol Pot's words, "Enemies attack and
torment us. From the east and from the west, they persist in pounding us and worrying us. If we are slow and
weak, they will mistreat us.". . .

On August 21, 1976, Pol Pot convened a meeting of
the "Party Center" (Central Committee) to formally
introduce the Four Year Plan to build socialism in agriculture, industry, health and welfare, education, and so
on. It was scheduled to take effect at the beginning of
1977. The plan had been actually inaugurated at an
"agricultural meeting" at the end of 1975 following
consultations between the party center and the various
zones. It had been unveiled again at a longer meeting
convened in late July. On both occasions Pol Pot had
presented the plan as a fait accompli; discussion of its
provisions was muted or nonexistent.

In essence, the plan sought to achieve socialism in
Cambodia within four years by collectivizing agriculture and industry and by spending money earned from
agricultural exports to finance agricultural production,
light industry, and eventually heavy industry as well.
Capital accumulation, ironically, was to occur in a society in which money, markets, and private property had
been abolished.

The plan embodied many of Pol Pot's idées fixes [obsessions]—collectivism, revolutionary will, autarky, and the empowerment of the poor, to name only four. Pol Pot saw the document as the means by which Cambodia could accelerate toward socialism. The unreality and sloppiness of most of its proposals reveal a blind faith in the possibilities of success. When these proposals were applied at great speed by a self-absorbed regime, it resulted in the deaths of tens of thousands of citizens. As lower ranking cadre and officials, fearful of reprisals, struggled to apply what they took to be the exigencies of the plan, they made unworkable demands on the people under them on whose behalf the revolution was ostensibly being waged. . . .

Pol Pot's Fixation with Rice Production

All the same, there were many obstacles to achieving independence-mastery. Cambodia had no exportable minerals, few educated workers, even fewer technocrats, and an insignificant industrial sector. This meant that exports were limited to agricultural products. Of these, the most important was rice, which had been the backbone of Cambodian exports since the 1920s. There was no way of escaping the past or the reality of resources: Rice exports became the key element in the Four Year Plan. Pol Pot placed an almost metaphysical value on rice, associating it intimately with the recently empowered rural poor. Even before the plan was promulgated, the party had launched the slogan "Three tons [of unhusked rice] per hectare," which soon became a national goal. The slogan itself, without acknowledgment, echoed a campaign launched in China by Vice Premier Hua Guofeng toward the end of 1975. The target figure of 3 tons per hectare suggests that the Cambodian leaders had not worked out any agricultural slogans or policies of their own and that what was good enough for

China would suffice for Cambodia as well.

This hastiness and lack of thinking are not surprising. Hardly any of the leaders of the party had ever planted, transplanted, and harvested rice to feed a family. Although they knew that the target of 3 tons a hectare could not be achieved through uncoordinated storming attacks [local gangs of revolutionary soldiers would force peasants to plant extra rice] even within the framework of the plan it was unrealistically high. Before 1970, yields in Cambodia had averaged less than 1 ton of unhusked rice per hectare. Most of this was mediocre, produced on family-owned plots without fertilizer or machinery. The party's slogan demanded that Cambodia's average yield be tripled at once, not in response to superior technology or material incentives but as testimony to a collectivized revolutionary will and the transferability of military zeal into the economic sphere. "Can we accomplish the Plan or not?" Pol Pot asked rhetorically. "The answer is that we can accomplish it everywhere; *the evidence for this* is our political movement" (emphasis added).

Forced Labor Kills Expendable City People

The northwest—comprising the provinces of Battambang and Pursat—was where the agricultural sections of the plan were to have the most effect. In a draft of the plan, a party spokesman referred to this zone as a "number one battlefield" for economic growth. In that zone, land scheduled for two rice crops was to increase from 60,000 hectares in 1977 to 200,000 hectares in 1980, making up 40 percent of the national total of double-cropped land. Over 140,000 hectares of uncultivated or unproductive land were to be brought under cultivation. All in all, the northwest was scheduled to provide 60 percent of Cambodia's rice exports between 1977 and 1980.

Most of the work in the northwest would be done by over one million April 17 people who had been evacuated from Phnom Penh and from the city of Battambang into rural areas in the zone. Over the next two years, these men and women were forced to hack rice fields, canals, dams, and villages out of malarial forests. Tens of thousands of them died from malnutrition, disease, executions, and overwork. These deaths, when they became known, distressed the authorities in Phnom Penh only to the extent that they indicated that "enemies" were at work behind the scenes. New people, because they were so numerous and "class enemies" of the revolution, were expendable. Many survivors recall a chilling aphorism directed mockingly at them by cadre: "Keeping [you] is no gain. Losing [you] is no loss."

Profiles · in · History

Terrorism and National Liberation

The Bombing of the King David Hotel

Menachem Begin

Menachem Begin was born in Poland in 1913. During his youth, he was a member of the militant Jewish youth group Betar. He was imprisoned by the Russians, who invaded Poland in 1941, but was released and immigrated to Palestine (then under British rule) in 1942.

When Begin arrived, he joined the Irgun Zvai Le'umi (National Military Organization), an underground organization dedicated to driving the British out of Palestine and creating a Jewish state that was to be called Israel in the region the Jews consider their rightful homeland. To achieve these aims, the Irgun and Begin were willing to commit acts of terrorism. Begin's fight was eventually successful; the British left Palestine and the new State of Israel was established by UN mandate in 1948. In 1977, Begin became prime minister of Israel. He shared the Nobel Peace Prize with Egyptian president Anwar Sadat for the peace negotiations they conducted in 1978–1979.

In the following excerpt, Begin describes the Irgun's most infamous act, the bombing of the King David Hotel in Jerusalem. The hotel was then serving as the British army headquarters in Palestine. The attack was a reprisal

Menachem Begin, *The Revolt*. New York: Nash, 1977. Copyright © 1951 by Menachem Begin. Reproduced by permission.

for British army raids on the Jewish community, the Yishuv, in Tel Aviv. While Begin claims that attempts were made to avoid the loss of life, the bombing of the hotel killed ninety-one people.

🐝   🐝   🐝

On the 1st July, 1946, two days after [General Evelyn] Barker's [British commander in Palestine] attack on the Jewish Agency, we received a letter from the Haganah [the Zionist defense council] Command which ran as follows:

"Shalom!

"(a) You are to carry out as soon as possible the Chick [the code name for the bombing of the British headquarters in Palestine] and the house of 'Your-slave-and-redeemer.' Inform us of the date. Preferably simultaneously. Do not publish the identity of the body carrying out the operation—neither directly nor by implication.

"(b) We are also preparing something—shall inform you of details in good time.

"(c) Tel Aviv [the main Jewish city, later capital of Israel] and neighbourhood must be excluded from all operations. We are all interested in protecting Tel Aviv—as the centre of Yishuv [the Jewish settlement in Palestine] life and our own work. If Tel Aviv should be paralysed by curfew and arrests as the result of an operation, we and our plans will also be paralysed. Incidentally, the important nerves of the other sides are not concentrated here. So—Tel Aviv is 'out of bounds' to Jewish forces."

When we received this letter we set about preparing "Operation Chick." We could not do it immediately. The Haganah's request that we attack the Hotel reached us several weeks after they had at first rejected the same plan. In the meantime a number of circumstances had changed. As a result, we had to carry out anew all the reconnaissance operations and reconsider the whole of the operational details. We were well aware that this was the largest of our operations to date and that it might turn out to be unique in the history of partisan wars of liberation. It is no simple matter to penetrate the very heart of the military government, to deliver a blow within the fortified headquarters of a heavily armed regime. I doubt if this operation had any precedent in history.

A Reprisal Is Necessary

We dared not fail. After the 29th of June, large sections of the people had been thrown into confusion. Barker's blow had been very severe. Defeatism raised its deathly head. People began to question our ability to fight the British regime. Many expressed their despair as to the outcome of any "struggle": "Who are we, what is our strength, that we should be able to stand up to the British Army?" These questions were pregnant with danger. They reflected the defeatism that is fatal to every war of liberation. We realised that Jewish self-confidence could be restored only by a successful counter-attack in reply to Barker's heavy blows. We were therefore greatly relieved by the request of the Haganah, and plunged with enthusiasm into a re-examination of every detail of the operation. We always planned every undertaking with infinite care. But to none of our many operations—except, perhaps, the later attack on Acre Fortress[1]—did we devote so much preliminary preparation as we did to "Operation Chick."

Giddy's [Giddy Paglin, head of operations for the Irgun] tremendous inventive and creative power were

1. a Crusader fortress in the Acre, an ancient city in Israel

called upon to the full. Innocent milk-cans became the bearers of high explosives. Their action was doubly assured. One mechanism determined the time of explosion—half-an-hour after the cans were left in position; the other secured the cans against any attempt at removal or dismantling.

A prime consideration was the timing of the attack. Two proposals were made: one for eleven a.m., the other for between four and five o'clock in the afternoon. Both plans were based on the same reasoning. The milk-cans could be brought into the Government wing of the building only by way of the "Regence Café" situated in the basement of the wing occupied by Barker and Shaw. In these morning and afternoon hours the Café was usually empty. At lunch-time it was filled with customers, among them civilian men and women as well as Army officers. It was essential that the attack be delivered at an hour when there were no customers in the Café.

Of the proposed hours, which both met this condition, we chose the earlier—11 A.M.—because it was easier then to coordinate our attack with that planned by the F.F.I. [Fighter's for the Freedom of Israel, also called the Stern Group] on the David Brothers Building—"Operation Slave and Redeemer." It was clear that these operations must be simultaneous: otherwise the one would interfere with the other.

Next we considered how to give the warnings so as to eliminate casualties. First, to keep passers-by away from the building, we decided to let off a small cracker-bomb, noisy but harmless. Then we chose three offices to receive a telephoned warning, which would be given as soon as our men had got away from the basement of the hotel. These three were: the King David Hotel management; the *Palestine Post*, and the French Consulate-General which is close to the Hotel. Finally, warning placards would be placed next to the milk-cans: "Mines. Do not Touch"—in case British experts should attempt to dismantle the explosives after our telephoned warning had been sent out.

Operation "Chick" Is Carried Out

Operation "Chick" was carried out exactly three weeks after we received the Haganah's instructions to execute it. During that time a number of meetings took place between us and the leaders of the Resistance Movement. Once the F.F.I. called for a postponement as they were not yet ready for their task. Twice or thrice we postponed the attack at the request of the Haganah Command. These postponements were very dangerous. Each time the number of people in the know increased. As I have already mentioned, participants in every operation were given a preliminary and detailed briefing on their task. In the case of the Hotel operation, a comparatively large number of men had already been briefed. Every new postponement was therefore liable to endanger not only the plan itself but also its participants. We consequently protested against these postponements, but resigned ourselves to them out of necessity. On July 19th, I received a note from Moshe Sneh [leader of the Haganah]:

"Shalom!

"My comrades have told me of the last talk. If you still respect my personal appeal, I ask you most earnestly to postpone the planned operations for a few more days."

We acceded to this request, and accepted the 22nd of July as the final date. But the F.F.I. again were unable to complete their preparations; and at the last moment it was decided to go ahead with the attack on the King David Hotel alone. Because of last-minute consultations, the time of attack was delayed by one hour and began at twelve o'clock instead of eleven.

The Assault Unit, under the command of the Jerusalem Gideon (dressed in the flowing robes of a hotel worker), executed the attack with great bravery and carried out their orders with absolute punctiliousness. They brought the milk-cans as far as the approach to the hotel. They then divided into two groups, one for the "break-through" and the other to "cover" the first. The first group took the milk-cans into the basement by way of the Regence Café. They overwhelmed the café employees and locked them in a side-room. These fifteen Arabs presented no surprise to our men: the peaceful subjection of the cooks and waiters—the only persons in the café at the time—was part of the plan. But our men were surprised by the sudden appearance of two British soldiers who, their suspicions being aroused, drew their revolvers. A clash was unavoidable. Both sides suffered casualties. Meanwhile the covering group outside had clashed with the British military patrols. In view of the nature of the operation our men had no machine-guns and had to fight with Sten guns and revolvers. However, the break-through party reached its objective. The commander of the operation himself set the time mechanism at thirty minutes and put up the warning placards. The Arab workers were then freed and ordered to run for their lives. They did not hesitate. The last man out was Gideon, who shouted "Get away, the hotel is about to blow up." At the moment the warning cracker-bomb was exploded outside the hotel and under cover of its smoke our men withdrew. The noise caused by the bomb and the unexpected shooting drove away all passers-by in the streets.

The Irgun Issues Warnings About the Bombing

At ten minutes past twelve, Gideon reached the spot at which our "telephonist" was waiting. She immediately telephoned the King David Hotel and warned them that explosives had been placed under the hotel and would go off within a short time. "Evacuate the whole building!"—she cried to the hotel telephone-operator. She then telephoned the office of the *Palestine Post* and announced—as was later testified by the *Palestine Post* telephonist—that "bombs have been placed in the King David Hotel and the people there have been told to evacuate the building." The third and final warning was given to the French Consulate, accompanied by advice to open the Consulate windows so as to prevent the effects of blast. The Consulate officials subsequently confirmed the receipt of the warning. They opened their windows wide, and the French Consulate building suffered no damage.

It was now twelve-fifteen. Gideon was counting the minutes. So far, everything had gone according to plan, except for the casualties we had suffered in the unexpected clash. The milk-cans were lodged in the basement under the Government wing of the hotel. All warnings had been delivered and received. The British had no doubt begun the evacuation and, if things had gone as before in similar circumstances, would very soon complete it. Only one question bothered him: would the explosives go off? Might not some error have been made in the mechanism? Would the building really go up? Would the documents be destroyed?

Each minute seemed like a day. Twelve-thirty-one, thirty-two. Zero hour drew near. Gideon grew restless. The half-hour was almost up. Twelve-thirty-seven. . . . Suddenly, the whole town seemed to shudder. There had been no mistake. The force of the explosion was greater than had been expected. Yitshak Sadeh, of the Haganah, had doubted whether it would reach the third or even the second floor. Giddy had claimed that, though only about 500 lbs. of explosives—a compound of T.N.T. and gelignite—had been put into the milk-cans, the confined space of the basement would heighten the force of the escaping gases, and the explosion would reach the roof. The milk-cans "reached" the whole height of the building, from basement to roof, six storeys of stone, concrete and steel. As the B.B.C. [British Broadcasting Corporation] put it—the entire wing of a huge building was cut off as with a knife.

The Bomb Causes Loss of Innocent Lives

But while our Assault Unit in the lion's den had done everything possible to ensure the timely evacuation of the hotel, others had taken a different line. For some reason the hotel was not evacuated even though from the moment when the warnings had been received there was plenty of time for every living soul to saunter out. Instead, the toll of lives was terrible. More than two hundred people were killed or injured. Among the victims were high British officers. We particularly mourned the alien civilians whom we had had no wish to hurt, and the fifteen Jewish civilians, among them good friends, who had so tragically fallen. Our satisfaction at the success of the great operation was bitterly marred. Again we went through days of pain and nights of sorrow for the blood that need not have been shed.

Ahmed Ben Bella's Terror Campaign Against French Rule in Algeria

Robert Merle

Ahmed Ben Bella, born in 1916, was the leader of the native resistance to French colonial administration in Algeria. Algeria had long been one of France's most valuable African colonies, and about 10 percent of the population was of European descent. Algerian Muslims, the vast majority of the population, were second-class citizens in the country. Ben Bella, who had been a soldier in the French army during World War II, found this situation intolerable. He rejected the program of gradual reform that was being promoted by old Algerian leaders. Instead, he organized the *Organisation Spéciale*—the Special Organization—to propagandize among poor Algerian Muslims for armed revolt. His revolt was eventually victorious; Algeria gained its independence in 1962. Ben Bella, however, was deposed in a coup in 1965, and lived in exile in Egypt until 1990, when he returned to Algeria.

In common with many leaders of nationalist movements who are in a weak position, Ben Bella justified as necessary

Robert Merle, *Ben Bella*, translated by Camilla Sykes. London: Michael Joseph, 1967.

"the propaganda of the deed." He first planned operations to kill his opponents among native Algerian leaders. He plotted bombings against the symbols of French rule. Finally, he organized a raid on the post office in Oran, hoping to finance his revolt by robbery. (Post offices in French Algeria functioned somewhat as banks.) French officials were able to link him with this raid and arrest him. In this excerpt from an interview, Ben Bella uses mild language to describe what was a violent campaign against French rule.

Robert Merle was born in French Algeria. A linguist, translator, and author of both fiction and nonfiction works, he served as liaison officer with the British army during World War II.

❦   ❦   ❦

O wing to the pressure of events, a crisis had blown up in the M.T.L.D.[1]; a split had widened between the leaders of the party and its more determined fighting members. The latter had obliged the leaders to form a secret organization, of which I became the chief. We called it the *Organisation Spéciale* [Special Organization]. It ended by becoming a party within a party, so different were its aims and its mentality to those of Messali [a moderate Algerian leader, who favored cooperation with the French]. He, in fact, was becoming more and more constitutional, and believed that thanks to the elections the situation would evolve and that we would eventually be able to make ourselves heard and gradually obtain more concessions from the colonial administration. Like all the young fighters of the *Organisation Spéciale*, I could only believe that his view was

1. the French abbreviation for Movement for the Triumph of Democratic Liberties, a party fighting for native Algerians' rights

an illusion. We were anxious to take action, as the events of Sétif[2] had convinced us that, sooner or later, it would be a question of using force, and that we must prepare ourselves for this.

Algerian Militants Reject Elections

The rigged elections of 1948, organized by the 'socialist' [French politician Edmond] Naegelen, emphatically confirmed our point of view. No parody of the democratic voting system has ever been conducted with such cynicism. The policy of nagging which followed served to enlighten us. It was as though the colonial administration bore the Algerians a grudge for having won the pure formality of the right to vote, and for having put it to all the trouble of having had to fake the election results. Every meanness which could be thought up by a colonial bureaucrat was practised against my brother Algerians. The Moorish cafés were closed down. Peasants were fined for riding their donkeys on the wrong side of the road. These small irritations accumulated the whole time, and created an atmosphere of hate. It was obvious that the object of these petty restrictions was to punish us for our inexcusable and tremendous 'presumption' in claiming the right to vote, even though these elections were always fixed beforehand. We were undergoing a system of punishment which in military parlance would be called 'a regaining of control'. The system was brutal, as well as niggling and petty; it was intended to make the 'native' once and for all 'know his place'—and his place was the lowest in the land.

Ben Bella Secretly Organizes Resistance

It was part of my work to go from village to village, visiting our militant supporters and persuading sympa-

2. Several dozen Europeans had been killed in an uprising in the Northern Algerian district of Sétif. The killings led to severe reprisals from French colonial authorities.

thizers to join our ranks. My visits were secret; I never stayed in hotels, but always with local people, and I went out very little. I discovered that peasant opinion was very similar to my own. As they did not know of the existence of the *Organisation Spéciale*, they could only judge the activities of the M.T.L.D. by the pronouncements of its leaders, with whom they were thoroughly disgusted. "Listen, my son," a peasant said to me one day, "do you know what happens if the administration finds out that one of us is a member of the M.T.L.D.? They send the police to drag him out of his house and beat and humiliate him in front of his wife; then they fling him into prison without trial. When he comes out, he is bullied by the *bachaga* and the *caïd*.[3] That is the system. We are crushed, oppressed, and ground underfoot. And after all this, the party talks to us of elections! Of what use are elections? To parade about among the French? To take part in their municipal councils, their assemblies, their political meetings? What would all this lead us to? To some minor progress, perhaps in a hundred years' time. But in a hundred years' time we will all be dead. No, my son, we don't want to hear any more about elections. What we want now is—guns."

Ordinary Algerians Desire Armed Revolt

We heard this kind of talk everywhere, and we did not fail to pass it on, with vehemence, to the leaders of our party. But it was impossible to shake them out of their 'wait-and-see' policy. Their attitude can only be described as one of readiness for flight; they shirked making any necessary decisions. The thought of armed rebellion against the colonial power scared them, and the idea of a general revolt did so even more. They kept on postponing vital decisions to some future date, and taking refuge mean-

3. local Algerian tribal rulers, used as puppets by the French colonial administration

while in constitutionalism. If only the elections had been genuine, and if only the power of the elected members had been real! Faced with the massive and hopeless oppression which weighed our people down, the party's parliamentary ambitions seemed ludicrous.

The party leaders were only aware of one aspect of the alienation of the masses from the party: membership had dwindled, and subscriptions were no longer coming in. Political parties have always existed on the contributions of the poor and humble, such as the *fellaheen* [poor Arabs who were generally menial laborers without land of their own], who make sacrifices to keep them going; it was these people who were now beginning to desert us in increasing numbers. I remember that at that time the finances of the M.T.L.D. had fallen so low that we sometimes had difficulty in paying our regular staff. . . .

The [M.T.L.D. Party] Congress of 1949 made some major decisions without the consent of these people. It decided that the party should place the major part of its funds at the disposal of the *Organisation Spéciale*. In order to make sure that this decision did not remain merely a dead letter, the Congress appointed me as chief political organizer of the party, as well as head of the *Organisation Spéciale*.

The *Organisation Spéciale* Neutralizes Its Enemies

The time had come for action. Our propaganda work was being considerably hampered at this time by vagrant bands recruited by the *caïds* and *bachagas* to terrorize the districts under their control. The best-known of these gangs was run by the *bachaga* Aït Ali, in Kabylia [the southern district of Algeria]. His men were thorough scoundrels, highway robbers who pillaged and murdered with complete impunity. These killers acted against our members in all cases where the administration did not wish to soil its hands, using the same methods which had operated against me at Marnia,[4] which I have already exposed. The *Organisation Spéciale*, emerging strengthened and invigorated from the 1949 Congress, decided to take action against these thugs. With some difficulty, permission to neutralize them was obtained from the party leaders. This was a police operation, rough but necessary, and it did much to change the atmosphere in Algeria.

If I remember rightly, it was at this time that the *Organisation Spéciale* decided to blow up the monument which had been erected by the authorities to the memory of the Emir Abd-el-Kader. He was a national hero who had fought for fifteen years to defend the independence of Algeria against the invader, and it seemed to us sacrilegious that the colonial administration should now claim him as an ally. The operation was not entirely successful, but nevertheless our attempt helped in large measure to clarify public opinion.

The party's lack of funds continued to paralyse our movements, and the young active members of the *Organisation Spéciale* decided that, at all costs, we must escape from this situation. We did not have the same careful bourgeois scruples about money as our leaders had, because we ourselves were completely disinterested. We told them: "There is no shortage of money in Algeria: we must get it from the banks and post offices, where there is plenty. Let us be consistent: if we are prepared to stake our lives in a violent attack against the occupier of our country, we must not hesitate to plunder his safes." The leaders finally agreed to our plan in principle, with many wry faces, and after having carefully absolved themselves of all responsibility.

4. Marnia is Ben Bella's home town. Officials had instigated a dispute between him and another Algerian, hoping he would be killed as a result.

The Raid on the Oran Post Office

The plan was to raid the Oran [the second largest city in Algeria] post office. Our intelligence had been thorough, and we reckoned to lay our hands on thirty million francs, which would have filled the party's coffers in one fell swoop and allowed us to purchase arms. In actual fact the haul was very much smaller.

The raid was very carefully organized. In order to deflect suspicion from our members, we decided to disguise the attack as a hold-up by Pierrot-le-Fou ["Pierrot the crazy," a French bank robber], whose exploits were filling the newspapers at that time. We chose fair-haired Algerians as our men for the job, dressed them in European clothes, and told them to speak with a Paris accent.

Our subterfuge was successful. The newspapers at once detected the hand of Pierrot-le-Fou, and commented with some surprise on the fact that he had now transferred his operations to North Africa. But our luck was not destined to hold, and an unbelievable series of infinitesimal mischances began to act against us.

The raiders had used a rather worn old suitcase to remove the bank-notes and, in the hurry of getting away, part of the metal fitting had caught on something, and a minute fragment had broken off and fallen onto the carpet of the black front-wheel drive car which they were using. This fragment, although very small, was found by the police investigators and preserved as a possible piece of incriminating evidence. However, time passed, no real clues materialized, and the inquiries came to a standstill. Then one day, an officer of the criminal police department, who had been taking part in the inquiries, was transferred to the department of *Renseignements Généraux* [the intelligence service of the police force]. This man was sent to search the house of one of our active members and took a fancy to a suitcase, which he decided to confiscate for his personal use. This minor act of plunder had serious results for us. When he got the suitcase home, the police officer had some difficulty in opening it: he looked at it more closely and noticed that a piece of metal was missing. Then he remembered the minute scrap of evidence which he had handled a few months earlier. He rushed off to the police station with the suitcase, where he proved that the broken fitting and the small piece of metal corresponded exactly. He realized in a flash that the Oran post office raid was no ordinary hold-up organized by Europeans, but an operation mounted by our party. Arrests and torture began from that moment and finally they got onto my trail.

Ben Bella Is Arrested

The first time I was nearly arrested was in February 1950, at Algiers Central Post Office. But I succeeded in pushing my way past the police, and took to my heels. I saw that they were following me, so I took my revolver from my pocket, brandished it over my head without firing it, and never stopped running until I saw that I had outdistanced them. Doubtless discouraged by the prospect of an exchange of shots, the police gave up, and I got away.

But it was only a brief respite. A month later they caught me in my hiding-place in Algiers; I had been denounced by a traitor.

The police had discovered the existence of our organization, but in the long run they only managed to arrest a few of our militant members, or 'shock troops'. They had, however, found out enough to be able to call it a plot, and of course they flattered themselves that it had been nipped in the bud and crushed.

As was to be expected, the party leaders took fright and dissociated themselves from our attempted *coup*. At the same time they conveyed to me, and to the men who were accused with me, that the case was to proceed without publicity.

We took good care to disobey these orders because, if our action was to make any sense, we had got to justify it by loudly proclaiming the underlying political motives. In consequence, we adopted a fighting attitude from beginning to end and reversed our position from that of accused to that of accusers, turning our trial into a trial of colonialism. We even kept up our aggressive action outside the law-court; from the prison to the court and back again, we sang our national hymn in unison, and at the tops of our voices. Every means, including pressure, threats and sanctions, was used to try to stop our singing. In the end, the police, who could not silence us, had to arrange to make us inaudible. They surrounded our prison van with an army of motor-cycle outriders, who raced their engines whenever we opened our mouths. Luckily for us, they had to stop when they came to the steps of the Palais de Justice [courthouse]; we never missed a chance to sing our hymn when entering or leaving the court, in the presence of the magistrates.

Yasir Arafat and Fatah

Neil C. Livingstone and David Halevy

Israel's War of Independence in 1948 brought victory for Jews living in what was then called Palestine, but it also meant that tens of thousands of Arab Palestinians were forced into exile. These displaced people looked to the neighboring Arab countries, such as Egypt, to destroy Israel and thus allow them to return to the land they had left. However, by the mid-1960s—and after two wars—it was evident that the Arab nations were unable to achieve the Palestinians' goal.

Inspired by the example of the Algerian National Liberation Front (FLN), which won independence after a war (1954–1962) with the colonial French government, Yasir Arafat decided to pursue an armed liberation struggle against Israel. Like the leaders of other national liberation movements, Arafat chose terror as a weapon to counter the Israeli's overwhelming military advantage. The following excerpt details Arafat's early life and the influences that led him to turn to terror as a tool of Palestinian national liberation.

Neil C. Livingstone has written frequently on the subject of terrorism. He is the president and chief executive officer of GlobalOptions, Inc., a risk management firm. David Halevy is a veteran Middle East correspondent who has contributed to *Time* magazine.

Neil C. Livingstone and David Halevy, *Inside the PLO: Covert Units, Secret Funds, and the War Against Israel and the United States.* New York: William Morrow, 1990.

❦   ❦   ❦

Early on the morning of Sunday, January 3, 1965, Aryeh Zizhik, an employee of Mekorot, Israel's national water company, discovered a suspicious object floating in a canal in the Belt Netofa Valley, part of the lower Galilee. The canal carried fresh water from the Jordan River more than two hundred miles to the Negev desert and was a vital element in Israel's program to "make the desert bloom." The diversion of the waters of the Jordan had been the main topic of debate at the 1964 Arab summit in Cairo and the target of bitter threats by the Arab governments, which vowed to destroy it.

Zizhik was ordered to close the canal gates and drain the water from a large section of the canal. A short time later explosives ordnance disposal (EOD) experts from Israel's border police arrived and approached the object, which turned out to be a plastic-covered rucksack, now lying on the bottom of the dry canal. Inside the rucksack were ten sticks of a powerful explosive known as gelignite and a detonator and batteries. The gelignite was Hungarian-made and of a type used frequently by regular units of the Syrian Army. The explosive device had not gone off because of flaws in its assembly, but had it done so, it would have caused considerable damage, especially if it had hit the canal locks or drifted downstream to the pumping stations.

Bedouin trackers quickly picked up the trail of the saboteurs, which led to the village of Araba and from there to the banks of the Jordan River, where the tracks stopped abruptly at the water's edge. The saboteurs had apparently crossed the river into Jordan, and it was assumed that they had probably entered Israel the same way.

Two days later a previously unknown organization called al-Fatah claimed credit for the operation. "It was," one PLO [Palestine Liberation Organization] official later claimed, "the first salvo of the Palestinian revolution." Indeed, for both Israel and the stateless Palestinians seeking a homeland, life would never be the same again.

Who Is Yasir Arafat?

Much of the information that appears in open sources about Yasir Arafat is contradictory and often erroneous, designed both to mythologize him and, in some cases, to hide his past from contemporary scrutiny. Mystery surrounds such details as the date and place of his birth, as well as why he changed his name.

Israeli intelligence files suggest that Arafat was born in 1928 in Cairo as Abed a-Rachman Abed a-Rauf Arafat al-Qudwah al-Husseini, although he has claimed on various occasions to have been born both in Gaza and in Jerusalem in a "house that was destroyed by the Jews." Alan Hart, Arafat's official biographer, also says that he was born in Cairo, but on August 24, 1929. His mother was a member of the prominent Abu-Saud family, which owned a house in Jerusalem, near the Western ("Wailing") Wall, that was knocked down by the Israeli government in 1969 in order to make way for the Western Wall plaza.

Early in life Arafat dropped his last name and changed his first name to Yasir. Why Arafat wanted to distance himself from his illustrious relative the grand mufti [the chief Islamic religious leader] of Jerusalem, Haj Amin al-Husseini, is not known. It is a surprising decision since al-Husseini was a direct descendant of Hussein, the grandchild of the Prophet Mohammed, and thus from one of the most celebrated families in all Islam. However, it may have something to do with the fact that al-Husseini had collaborated with Adolf Hitler during World War II.

A Man with Many Names

At various times later, after becoming a revolutionary, Arafat used sobriquets [made-up names] to conceal his real identity, such as Abu Amar, Abu Mohammed, the Doctor, Fauzi Arafat, and Dr. Husseini. The one he used most often was Abu Amar, which he subsequently adopted as his nom de guerre. He may have chosen Amar because in Arabic, *al-Amar* means "the command of God." There is a passage in the Koran [the holy book of Islam] (Sura [Chapter] 17:85) which says, "They put questions to you about the Spirit. Say: 'the Spirit is at my Lord's command (al-Amar).'" Most senior PLO members have taken on noms de guerre beginning with "Abu." Traditionally, in Arabic-speaking societies, when a man has his first son, his friends and neighbors thereafter refer to him as Abu (meaning "father of") and the name of the newborn child. If one is disgraced (in Arab societies) by having only daughters and no sons, he is often referred to behind his back as Abu al-Banat, meaning the "father of daughters." Although Arafat is not married and has no children and therefore is not the "father of" anyone, the name Abu served as a convenient means of portraying himself as a strong and virile man, which is greatly esteemed in his culture. The adoption of such names also serves to make it more difficult for foreign—initially Arab—intelligence services to keep track of various Palestinian figures, since noms de guerre create a good deal of confusion. For example, in the Arab world Musa and Daoud (David) are very common names; thus, the names Abu Musa and Abu Daoud told authorities very little about the real identities of the men. There are many Abu Amars in the Palestinian movement, including Jamel Suraani, who also serves on the PLO's Executive Committee with Arafat.

According to some sources, Arafat's father originally moved in the early 1920's to Cairo, where he lived off the comfortable income he received from the family properties in Egypt, Gaza, and Jerusalem. He had seven children from his first marriage: daughters Inam, Yosra, and Khadija and sons Gamal, Mustafa, Fatchi, and Yasir. In view of the date of his father's move, there is little doubt that Arafat was born in Cairo and attended elementary school there. Those who recall the family, however, say that they maintained their Palestinian identity and made little attempt to assimilate into Egyptian society.

Arafat Involved in Politics from an Early Age
There are unverified reports that Arafat's father and brother Gamal were members of the Moslem Brotherhood [a radical Islamic organization in Egypt] What is known is that Arafat's family was highly politicized and that Yasir became immersed in Palestinian politics at a very early age. In 1946 Haj Amin al-Husseini, the former grand mufti, arrived in Cairo, from Berlin, with his cousin, Palestinian nationalist leader Abed al-Kader al-Husseini. Al-Husseini spent more than a year in Cairo rebuilding his Palestinian constituency, before moving in October 1947 to Beirut, where he lived until his death in 1974.

They met with Arafat's brother Gamal, who subsequently joined Abed al-Kader al-Husseini's forces during the 1947–1948 war. Gamal remained active in Palestinian politics and served as secretary of the "All-Palestinian Government," which was formed in Gaza on September 22, 1948, and headquartered in Cairo. He also served as personal secretary to the aging Palestinian "prime minister" Ahmed Hilmi, the manager of the Arab Bank in Jerusalem.

It is presumed that Arafat met with the two Palestinian leaders during their stay in Cairo, and there is a report that he subsequently became a personal aide to Abed al-Kader al-Husseini. Arafat also claims to have fought with al-Husseini's forces around Jerusalem in 1947–1948, but again there is no confirmation of this. What is known is that in 1951 he began studying engineering at Cairo's Fuad I University, where he rapidly became involved in student politics and was known as a Palestinian agitator.

Arafat Studies Warfare

Arafat reportedly paid little attention to his studies and spent much of his time training Egyptian and Palestinian students in irregular warfare tactics. It was in this context that he first met Salah Khalaf (Abu Iyad). Although Abu Iyad recalls that he didn't care for Arafat's Egyptian accent, "I was impressed by his obvious leadership qualities as I watched him training the students. He was very dynamic. Very tough. Very passionate." The two men gradually formed a bond that has existed to this very day. Indeed, their roles really have not changed very much. Arafat remains the front man, the politician, the leader; Abu Iyad is the dark visage in the background, the tactician and "enforcer," the brooding intellectual.

Both men subsequently became active in the General Union of Palestinian Students (GUPS), and Arafat was elected president of the organization in 1952. It was as president of GUPS that Arafat first began to espouse publicly his notion of "an independent Palestine liberation movement." During this period Arafat and Abu Iyad drew around them other young Palestinians, active in GUPS at Egyptian universities, who were also committed to the notion of armed struggle as the means of achieving self-determination and regaining their homeland: Khalil al-Wazir (Abu Jihad), Mohammed Yussef al-Najjar (Abu Yussef), Kamal Adwan, Machmud Abbas

(Abu Mazan), and Farouk Qadoumi. Together with Arafat and Abu Iyad, these five men were to become the founding fathers of Fatah and later were instrumental in the takeover of the PLO.

Three of the seven have already become casualties of the struggle. Al-Wazir (Abu Jihad) was killed by Israeli commandos in Tunis on April 16, 1988, and Najjar and Adwan died in an Israeli raid on Beirut on April 10, 1973.

Even in the early 1950's Arafat was an ascetic individual who neither smoked nor drank and had little, if any, life beyond "the struggle." He had no known liaisons with women or other men and associated almost exclusively with other Palestinian radicals. In 1956, on the eve of the Suez crisis, he was graduated with a degree in civil engineering. A short time later he and some of his Palestinian associates enrolled in an Egyptian Army explosives ordnance disposal course, and when he completed the instruction, he was made a second lieutenant in the Egyptian Army. During the subsequent Suez crisis Arafat was part of a commando battalion that saw some limited action. However, he spent most of his time removing mines at Port Said [a port city in Egypt]. For his part, Abu Iyad spent the war guarding a bridge in the center of Cairo.

Arrested in Egypt

In late 1956 or early 1957 Arafat was arrested by Egyptian security services as a political agitator, allegedly because of his ties to the Moslem Brotherhood. He was released from jail several months later and along with Qadoumi and Abu Jihad, departed for Kuwait. Al-Najjar, Adwan, and Abbas went to Qatar. Abu Iyad moved to Gaza, where he became a teacher. They all agreed to rendezvous again in the future, when the time was right, in order to form a revolutionary organization dedicated to armed struggle against Israel.

During the late 1950's Arafat remained active as a student leader, attending numerous international conferences as a member of the Sudanese delegation. Short (five feet four inches) and heavyset, Arafat wore cheap European suits and lifts in his shoes. He had a small mustache and routinely wore dark glasses, which became something of his trademark. He was a fiery orator who thumped the podium and waved his arms when he spoke. At student conferences he routinely demanded the expulsion of the Israeli delegation if one was in attendance. During this time Arafat probably supported himself with payments from two intelligence services, the Egyptian Muchabarat and the Syrian Deuxième Bureau.

It is believed that Arafat and his colleagues from their university days in Cairo were behind the establishment of a small monthly that appeared in Beirut in 1958 entitled *Falestinuna: Nada el-Chiat* ("Our Palestine: The Call of Life"), which was edited by Tufiq Khuri. The publication had some ties to the Moslem Brotherhood but was chiefly concerned with promoting the cause of an independent Palestinian state.

The Founding of Fatah

In 1959 Arafat, together with two partners, opened his own construction business in Kuwait. Their timing could not have been better. It was just at the beginning of the oil boom and at a time when the states around the Persian Gulf were starting to nationalize the oil companies in the region. Arafat's company secured Kuwaiti government contracts and built government facilities, roads, and housing. Arafat used his extensive ties within the Palestinian community to win still more contracts. In a relatively short period of time he was able to amass a modest personal fortune. Once he became fully involved in Palestinian nationalist politics, he sold his shares in the company to his partners and left Kuwait.

Fatah was born the same year Arafat started his business venture. Abu Iyad remembers the occasion:

> On October 10, 1959, a small group of us met in a discreet house in Kuwait to hammer out the organizational structures of Fatah. More meetings with other participants took place over the following days, always in the greatest secrecy. There were fewer than twenty of us in all, representatives of underground groups from various Arab countries and beyond, coming together to centralize our activities for the first time. This limited congress marked the formal creation of what was to become the most powerful national liberation movement Palestine had ever known.

The name *Fatah* is short for Harkat al-Tachrir al-Watanni al-Falestinia, or Palestine Liberation Movement; in reverse order its acronym is FATAH, which, in Arabic, means "conquest" or "victory." The word "Fatah" appears in a famous passage from the Koran (Sura 61:13): "Help from Allah and a speedy victory [Fatah]."

Arafat Inspired by Algerian Independence

Arafat moved to Beirut the following year and divided his time [struggle] between working as an engineer and revolutionary politics. In 1962 the FLN [Algerian National Liberation Front] rebels in Algeria signed the Avignon Agreements, providing for the independence of Algeria. No event more captured the imagination of the young Palestinian revolutionaries than the defeat of the French in Algeria. Arafat, Abu Iyad, and the others all are steeped in the literature of the Algerian revolt. Revolutionary writers like black psychiatrist Franz Fanon, who spoke of the "liberating influence of violence," had a great impact on them. According to Abu Iyad, "Franz Fanon was one of my favorite authors. In his *Wretched of the Earth*, which I read and reread countless times, he said that only a people who doesn't fear the guns and tanks of the enemy is capable of fighting a revolution to the finish. By that he meant the Algerian nationalists would never have started anything if they had taken into account the balance of power at the time they launched their insurrection." In addition to Fanon, Arafat and Abu Iyad embraced the works of [Chinese Communist leader] Mao Zedong, Vietnamese General Vo Nguyen Giap, and [French radical writer] Régis Debray, not to mention the mythology and symbolism that surrounded [Latin American revolutionary] Che Guevara. Over the years they saw to it that the works of Mao, Giap, and Debray were translated into Arabic and regularly reprinted in Palestinian publications such as *Falistinuna* ("Our Palestine"), the official organ of Fatah, and *el-Thoura el-Falestinia* ("The Palestinian Revolution").

Nevertheless, while the example of Algeria served as an important beacon to Arafat and his lieutenants, they knew that there were substantial differences between the Algerian experience and their own unfolding struggle. Unlike French-dominated Algeria, Israel was not an outdated vestige of colonialism, but rather a young and energetic nation led by men and women who themselves had fought against and, for all intents and purposes, defeated a colonial power, in this case Great Britain. Whereas the French colonizers of Algeria could always return to France, the Israelis had no place to retreat to; for them it would be a fight to the bitter end.

Fatah has been led, in effect, by Arafat since 1964, when he began to emerge as "first among equals," although it was not until April 15, 1968, that he was appointed by Fatah's Central Committee the "official spokesman and representative" of Fatah.

The Fatah operation to blow up the Israeli canal that was discovered on January 3, 1965, was the first independent guerrilla action taken against Israel by the Palestinians, and it rapidly established Fatah as the principal shock troops of the Palestinian Revolution.

The Struggle to Free Northern Ireland

Sean O'Callaghan

Sean O'Callaghan rose through the ranks of the Irish Republican Army (IRA), eventually becoming the leader of the IRA's southern command. Since the 1920s, the IRA had used terror tactics in the fight to bring Northern Ireland, part of the United Kingdom, into the Republic of Ireland. The conflict was religious as well as political; most who wanted a united Irish Republic were Roman Catholic, while the Protestants of Northern Ireland wanted to remain part of Great Britain.

O'Callaghan was born in 1954 to a Catholic family heavily involved in IRA activity. He joined the organization in 1970, at the age of fifteen. During his time in the IRA, O'Callaghan took part in numerous terrorist attacks and committed two murders. He eventually became disillusioned with the IRA and became an informer, giving information about terrorist activities to the Irish and British governments.

In the excerpt, O'Callaghan illustrates the hatred that IRA members had for the Protestants of Northern Ireland. It is this hatred that causes him to lose faith in the goals of the IRA. Rather than a romantic struggle to free the Irish nation from British rule, O'Callaghan came to see the conflict as an ugly fight between misguided religious groups.

❧   ❧   ❧

I was born in 1954 in Tralee, County Kerry, in the Irish Republic. It was and still is an area with a strong republican tradition. After the treaty and the formation of the Irish Free State [later the Republic of Ireland] in 1922 the IRA [Irish Republican Army] and the new Free State Army fought a bitter civil war. That war was conducted with great savagery in Kerry. Less than three miles from my parents' house, eight IRA prisoners were blown to pieces by government forces in an officially sanctioned reprisal for the earlier IRA murder of a Free State Army officer.

Civil war bitterness was still very much alive in parts of Kerry in the 1950s. My father's side of the family was steeped in that tradition. He and his brother, active IRA men, were interned without trial in the Curragh military camp in the early 1940s. My father, several aunts, and other family members have remained lifelong activists and supporters of the republican movement. That was the tradition and the family background into which I was born.

An Ordinary Family

We were an ordinary working class family. We stood out in no regard other than that my father was a member of a small, essentially secret organization which still harbored dreams of a 32-county republic.[1] They be-

---

1. The island of Ireland has six British-ruled counties in the north and twenty-six counties in the Irish Republic.

lieved that such a republic would only come about by armed force. Occasionally I came across guns, and once explosives, hidden in the house. Sometimes there were meetings in the house or in my grandmother's. We were always sent somewhere else when anything of that nature was taking place but we had at least a vague idea that something exciting or dangerous was happening. We knew that nothing of this was ever to be repeated to our friends.

Like the great mass of Irish people I was educated in my early years at school by nuns and Christian Brothers. The Brothers had a fierce nationalist ethos. They saw themselves as the moral guardians of nationalist Ireland. It was a world of Gaelic games [traditional Irish sports], the Irish language, and endless songs and stories about noble Irish patriots and treacherous English. The treachery of the English was at the root of all of Ireland's ills.

Sectarian Violence

The 1916 rebellion [the uprising which eventually led to the independence of the twenty-six counties of the Irish Republic] was celebrated with great gusto in 1966, when I was 12 years old. RTE [Radio Telefis Eireann] television indulged in an orgy of adulation. Schools had special screenings of films on the rising. We played mock games of Irish versus the British. I always wanted to be James Connolly, the republican socialist executed by the British after the surrender of the rebels. Less than two years after these celebrations the civil-rights movement in Northern Ireland burst onto our television screens. In reality we understood little about the issues, but our sympathies were firmly with the Catholics in Northern Ireland. When sectarian violence broke out in Belfast [the capital of British-ruled Northern Ireland] in 1969 there was a huge outpouring of emotion in the Republic. Soon Catholic refugees were being billeted [housed] in local houses, church property, and the army barracks.

The IRA split, and the Provisional IRA was formed: an event which I now regard as the greatest tragedy in modern Irish history. That was not how I felt at the time, of course. I was 15 years old in 1970 and could not wait to enlist. My political views were certainly to the left of the leadership of the movement. Some of the overt militarism, bordering on fascism, did worry me. I saw the Provisionals as rather like a popular front which would sweep away partition and the British presence. We would then have a realignment of the Left in Irish politics. After that it was full steam down the road to the socialist republic. There you have the sum total of the political literacy of a 15-year-old would-be Irish revolutionary.

Like most others of my age in the Republic I knew nothing of Protestants or unionists other than that they were known as the Ascendancy. They stole the land from the Catholics and persecuted them. The Protestant working class in Northern Ireland were simply dupes of the unionist ruling classes and the British government. Our naivete and ignorance was incredible. We would throw the British out and then the poor stupid prods [Protestants] would see the error of their ways and join us in a new utopian Ireland. In truth we gave little or no consideration to the question of what to do with Protestants. We were ready to fight against the British just like our forefathers. This time we would finish the business. British rule in Ireland would end for all time.

I joined the IRA in Tralee. My family background was such that I had little difficulty in joining—it was positively expected. It was not long before young IRA recruits in Northern Ireland were coming to Kerry for training in the use of weapons and explosives. Even though I was very young I found myself actively involved in this part of IRA activity. Needless to say, school appeared pretty boring by comparison and I soon lost interest in it.

The IRA recruits from Northern Ireland were in the main ordinary young men such as you would find in any British city, town, or rural area. They wore the same clothes, listened to the same music, and followed the same soccer clubs. They were more likely to spend their time arguing about the merits of [British soccer clubs] Manchester United or Liverpool than politics. That came later, after exposure to the Provisional ideologues in Long Kesh and other prisons.

They saw their duty as protecting their areas—Catholic ghettos in Belfast and Derry—from attack by Protestants. The Provisional IRA was forged out of inter-communal sectarian warfare [violent conflict between Catholics and Protestants]. The vast majority of the recruits had no coherent political outlook. They mainly despised politics. Youthful fascination with guns and bombs and a desire to get even with prods: that was their motivation. Ill-educated, ill-equipped, they were easy meat for the simple answer. The hard leadership of the Provisional IRA, mainly older men who had waited all their lives for the opportunity, gave them the guns and told them the Brits and unionists were to blame for all their problems.

A Sense of Belonging

The IRA gave these young men a sense of belonging, status in their community, and a purpose, a cause to believe in and to fight and die for. These were young men without much hope of employment who had seen their communities devastated in sectarian attacks. Now that they were hitting back their pride and dignity was re-

stored. It would be utterly wrong to see these young men universally as lurid, evil psychopaths. That they carried out the most awful acts of violence is beyond question. But the real blame lies with their leadership: the old republican/nationalists who instilled discipline, obedience, and a reverence for republican structures and traditions that allowed young men to kill even former friends for minor transgressions of the republican code.

On April 20, 1972, I was preparing bomb equipment for a training camp due to begin within days. In the shed where I had been working seconds before, there was a major explosion. I escaped from the blast with just a few cuts and minor bruises but I was arrested and charged with possession of explosives. While I was on remand in Limerick prison the Dublin government introduced the non-jury special criminal court which sentenced me to six months. That was the sort of sentence IRA prisoners could expect in those days: there was still a lot of sympathy in the Republic. The British Embassy had been burned down in Dublin following Bloody Sunday[2] in Derry.

When I was released I settled back into the same routine. One IRA meeting in Kerry in that period sticks in my mind. It was attended by a Dominican priest who came from Northern Ireland. There were perhaps thirty people present. The priest told us that British soldiers were raping Catholic women in Belfast. I did not really believe him, reasoning that if such activity was common the huge media circus then covering Northern Ireland could not miss it. Such pep talks hyped up the hate and allowed people to excuse the most awful atrocities committed by their own side.

In June 1973 I was sent to Donegal [an Irish county] to work in an IRA bomb factory. The idea was for me to get experience and then train others so that more such factories could be set up further south. Like most IRA schemes in those days it never quite came to full fruition. I was soon back in Kerry but this time I was working for IRA General Headquarters Staff, running a training camp. Many IRA men who later became well-known figures passed through that camp. Some are dead, others are in jail, others, I suppose, have long since left the IRA.

Murdering a Police Detective
In May 1974 I was sent to the Mid Ulster [Northern Ireland] Brigade of the IRA. On May 2, along with up

2. On January 30, 1972, British troops opened fire on Catholic civil rights marchers, killing thirteen.

to forty IRA men from the East Tyrone Brigade, I took part in an attack on an army/UDR [Ulster Defense Regiment] base at the Deanery in Clogher, County Tyrone. There was a heavy gun battle which lasted up to twenty minutes before we withdrew. We made our way to safe houses over the border in Monaghan. It was not until we listened to the early morning radio news that we heard that a UDR Greenfinch [a female member of the UDR] named Eva Martin had been killed. It would be wrong to say that any of us were disappointed at the news.

I stayed in Tyrone until August of 1975. During that period I took part in about seventy attacks, mainly against members of the security forces. In one of those attacks, I along with two others murdered a detective inspector in the RUC [Royal Ulster Constabulary, or police force] special branch [intelligence unit of the RUC] called Peter Flanagan. We shot him dead in a public house in Omagh, County Tyrone. The two people who carried out this murder with me were both younger than me. Both were from Belfast. The driver was little more than a young girl. The other was 17 years old and had escaped from youth custody in Belfast while charged with murdering a soldier. He was arrested in 1975 and charged with attempted murder. He was sentenced to life imprisonment and is still in custody today [1997]. He was transferred to Northern Ireland and will probably be released in the next year or so. He has never been charged with the murder which he committed with me.

By the time that I murdered Flanagan doubts were already forming in my mind about the real nature of the Provisional IRA. IRA volunteers in Tyrone were on the whole far more sectarian than I was or ever could be. Their Catholicism was of a virulent and hatefilled brand. It is, in retrospect, hard to see how it could have been otherwise. Militant Irish nationalism and Irish Catholicism have a deep and complex relationship, nowhere more so than in rural areas of Northern Ireland like Tyrone, Fermanagh, and Armagh.

During this period I was involved in recruiting new IRA volunteers. One of our main safe houses was a parochial house [building belonging to the local Catholic church or parish] outside Omagh. Sometimes we used that house to initiate new members. Imagine the effect on a young uneducated country lad brought to his parochial house under cover of darkness to be inducted into the IRA. Try telling him that the Church was not on his side. One of the local priests usually called on another house in that area where I and other IRA men often stayed. He took great delight in asking us to relate our latest escapades. He was also forever passing on information about local Protestants: usually members or ex-members of the UDR or RUC. At least one of these was later murdered by the Provisional IRA.

A War Against Protestants

This was, in reality, a war against Protestants. There was a deep, ugly hatred, centuries old, behind all of this. The prods had the better farms, the better jobs that belonged by right to the Catholics, and they wanted them. If I wanted to attack a British army patrol or barracks, the local Provos wanted to shoot a part-time UDR or police reservist. They wanted to murder their neighbors. They wanted to drive the Protestants off the land and reclaim what they believed was their birthright. Gradually the reality was getting through to me. This was no romantic struggle against British imperialism but a squalid sectarian war directed against the Protestant people of Northern Ireland.

In March or April of 1975, I was in a flat [apartment] in Monaghan town. The flat was a base for IRA men from the East Tyrone Brigade. That evening there were perhaps eight people, all full-time IRA activists, all on the run from Northern Ireland. I was making tea when a news item on the television about the death of an RUC woman in a bomb explosion was greeted with, "I hope she's pregnant and we get two for the price of one."

I felt utterly sickened and revolted. More so even when I realized who had spoken—a Tyrone man who was second in command of the Provisional IRA and a man I held in the highest regard; a man to whom I had thought seriously about addressing my doubts and fears. I went to another room where I just wanted to cry my eyes out. That man later became the chief of staff of the Provisional IRA. He was chief of staff when the present peace process began. Small wonder that I have serious doubts about the Provisional IRA's commitment to peace.

4

Profiles · in · History

Ideological
Terrorists

Carlos the Jackal: International Revolutionary

Ovid Demaris

Carlos the Jackal was exposed to revolutionary politics at an early age. Carlos—his real name was Ilich Ramírez Sánchez—enjoyed a privileged childhood in Caracas, Venezuela, in the early 1950s. His father was a wealthy physician who, despite his wealth, admired Communist revolutionaries. His mother looked after Carlos's education in languages and cultures when he was a young child. Later, his father sent him to Cuba and the Soviet Union to receive indoctrination in revolutionary Marxism.

After a few years at the University of Moscow, Carlos was expelled from the Soviet Union for spending more time drinking and chasing women than studying. Yet after his expulsion he lived up to his revolutionary training by becoming one of the world's most wanted terrorists. His fluency in several languages, coupled with abundant financial support from his parents, enabled Carlos to form terrorist networks around the world. In this excerpt, the journalist and crime writer Ovid Demaris shows how Carlos teamed up with German leftists to commit a daring assault on a 1975 meeting of OPEC, the Organization of Petroleum Exporting Countries, during which Carlos and his followers killed three men in cold blood. Carlos was tried and convicted in absentia of the murder of French intelligence agents in 1975, but was not captured until 1994. He is currently serving a life sentence in a French prison.

🐘 🐘 🐘

Sunday, December 21, 1975, was bitterly cold in Vienna. The city lay under a thick mantle of snow. Beginning on Friday that week, there had been an exodus to ski resorts for the Christmas holiday. Even [police inspector Anton] Tichler, who was working his last shift that morning before his retirement, was planning on taking his wife to Switzerland when he came off duty at one o'clock.

Eleven oil ministers and their delegations had convened at 10:50 A.M. with an agenda that included questions concerning the fixing of a new oil price. A group of journalists had assembled in the lobby downstairs to await developments. Just outside the front door, a uniformed policeman stood talking to a correspondent for an American publication.

At about 11:00 A.M., five young men and a woman, all carrying Adidas sports bags, came to the door and asked the correspondent if the conference was still in progress. Although he had no reason for suspicion, the correspondent watched them wend their way across the small lobby to the far flight of stairs. The one who had addressed the correspondent appeared to be the leader. He wore a Basque beret and an open white trench coat over a brown leather jacket. He was above average height and had long, curly hair, with wide sideburns down to his jawline, a moustache, and just the beginning of a goatee. As he turned sideways to wait for the others, his silhouette reminded the reporter of Che Guevara. The woman, who seemed barely out of her teens and very petite, had pulled a gray woolen ski cap so tightly over her head that it completely covered her hair. The last man to disappear behind the red steel door was small and dark, with a moustache and long black hair that curled up on his neck. He wore a big fur hat. It occurred to the correspondent that they were an unlikely group for OPEC [Organization of Petroleum Exporting Countries] people, but it was only a passing thought, certainly not anything worth repeating to the policeman.

The Most Famous Terrorist in the World

What he did not know, of course, was that the young man in the beret was Ilich Ramírez Sánchez, who at that moment was the most famous—and most wanted—terrorist in the world. Known universally by the pseudonym of Carlos Martínez Torres, the world press, in imitation of British journalists, had taken to calling him "The Jackal," after the main character in Frederick Forsyth's thriller *The Day of the Jackal*. If anyone truly epitomized the mobility and diversity of international terrorism it was this twenty-six-year-old multilingual Venezuelan. His escapades, as we shall see, revealed connections between terrorist groups in Asia, the Middle East, Africa, Europe, and South America. Among his known exploits were the bombing of Le Drugstore in Paris, the firing of RPG-7 missiles at an El Al airliner at Orly Airport [in Paris], the murder of two French intelligence officers and the Lebanese informer who had brought them to his Latin Quarter apartment, and the plotting of some of the most bizarre terrorist ventures in recent years. As a good luck charm that day, he wore a light blue roll-neck shirt, a gift from Dr. George Habash, his mentor and leader of the Popular

Front for the Liberation of Palestine (PFLP), one of
the most radical of the terrorist groups constituting the
Arab Rejection Front, which has sworn never to nego-
tiate with Israel.

The girl in the ski cap was Gabriele Kroecher-
Tiedemann, a twenty-three-year-old member of West
Germany's Baader-Meinhof gang [a group of revolutionary terrorists], whose terroristic activities had begun at an early age. Identified in a Berlin bank robbery
in February 1972, she was apprehended fifteen months
later after a gun battle with police. She was sentenced
to eight years in prison, but on March 3, 1975, she and
four other prisoners were flown to Aden, the capital of
South Yemen, as part of the ransom paid by the government for the release of Peter Lorenz, the leader of
West Berlin's Christian Democratic party, who had
been kidnapped by the Second of June Movement, a
younger offshoot of the Baader-Meinhof gang. Her
presence in Vienna marked her first public appearance
since receiving asylum in Aden.

Upstairs on the second floor, at precisely that moment, Tichler was telling [police inspector Josef] Janda
about his retirement plans. Both men were in plain
clothes and each was armed with a lightweight Walther
PPK automatic in a quick-draw holster. They were
standing in the anteroom near the sliding glass door, in
animated conversation, while inside the reception room
Edith Heller was struggling to stay awake in a room with
a dozen people smoking and chatting all around her.

There was a buzz and she turned to the small telephone switchboard to the right of her desk. "Good
morning, OPEC," she said in English. Tichler chose
that moment to walk toward the elevators. When
Heller looked up from her switchboard, men with guns
were swarming through the place. Tichler, she noticed
through the open glass door, was standing by the eleva-

tors with his hands up, and a young man in a Basque beret, whom she would later describe as "a tall, handsome man with curly brownish-blond hair," was pointing a Beretta machine pistol at his midsection. Then all hell broke loose.

Shots were fired and people in the reception room scrambled behind chairs and a black leather couch. Someone motioned for Heller to drop behind her desk, which she did, taking the telephone with her. There is no record at the Federal Police Directorate of her call, but people crouching on the floor beside her marveled at her courage when she screamed into the phone, "This is OPEC! They're shooting all over the place! OPEC! OPEC! This is OPEC!" Then she saw a pistol only inches away, and before she could see the face of the terrorist leaning over the desk, the gun went off and a bullet passed straight through the telephone into the floor. Two more shots destroyed the switchboard. Ears ringing from the shots, Edith Heller could not believe she was still alive.

The Murder of Police Inspector Tichler

Anton Tichler was not that fortunate. As a young policeman, he had been taught a special judo hold to disarm a man holding a weapon at close range. Under the best of conditions, it was a risky maneuver. It required great speed and strength, not to mention courage. For those who knew Tichler, there was no doubt that he was a proud and brave man. Yet Janda was shocked when he saw Tichler seize the barrel of the Beretta machine pistol. For a moment it looked like the old man might succeed in wresting the weapon out of the surprised terrorist's hands. But the thickset young man recovered quickly. Now both men were fighting for their lives. Tichler held on as long as he could, but it was an unequal contest. With a violent twisting motion, Carlos wrenched the weapon out of Tichler's hands, the movement sending both men staggering in opposite directions like contestants letting go in a tug-of-war.

As the momentum carried Carlos into the reception room, Tichler stumbled toward one of the elevators just as the doors were opening. What happened next was witnessed by the coffee-trolley lady standing in the elevator facing Tichler. From the expressions on their faces, both were terrified. There was no question that Tichler knew he was in serious trouble. Just as he was stepping into the elevator, Gabriele came up behind him and asked in English, "Are you a policeman?"

"Yes," said Tichler, as he began to raise his hands over his head without turning to face the girl, who at that moment was taking careful aim at the back of his neck. The bullet entered just below the hairline, and Tichler dropped at her feet, dying. With a motion of her gun, she sent the terrified coffee-trolley lady screaming into the reception room, to hide under Edith Heller's desk. Gabriele then pulled Tichler's body into the elevator and with a perverse theatrical touch, she sent it down to the ground floor. A Lenin axiom: "The product of terror is terror." Tichler's pistol was still in its fast-draw holster, unfired, when he was found.

The Terrorists Kill Two Who Resist

Ala Hassan Saeed al-Khafari, the Iraqi oil minister's bodyguard, was also a proud man. It did not take this tall, slender young man long to decide on a course of action. Just as Gabriele turned away from the elevator, Hassan grabbed her right arm and tried to twist the gun out of her hand. For Janda, who had passively witnessed Tichler's fate, there was no question that Hassan was stronger and quicker than Tichler and that the girl was weaker than Carlos, but it was still a futile gamble. As soon as Gabriele realized that he might get the best of her, she reached inside her clothing with her left hand, pulled out a second pistol, and shot Hassan in the face.

At that moment, Carlos grabbed Janda by the arm and ran him down the corridor leading to the conference room, firing shots into the ceiling as they went until bullets hit the wiring, extinguishing the corridor lights. Carlos pushed Janda into a staff office and closed the door. Making his way cautiously down the darkened corridor, lit only by dim emergency lights, he stopped to investigate another office only to come face to face with Yousef Ismirli, a member of the Libyan delegation.

There was madness in the air that morning. Ismirli's first impulse when he saw Carlos was to yank at his machine pistol so fiercely that it came out of his grasp. Only the shoulder strap prevented Ismirli from gaining complete control of the weapon. But again it was a hopeless gesture. Carlos pulled a pistol from his waistband and in a fit of rage fired five times—one of the bullets passing through Ismirli's body struck the right arm of a member of the Kuwaiti delegation.

The first thing Janda did was to hide his pistol and holster in a desk drawer. Then he telephoned for assistance. The taped emergency call was timed at 11:45 A.M. and the shots that killed Ismirli can be heard on the recording. . . .

The First International Terrorist

Before getting too deeply enmeshed in the convolutions of Middle East politics, let us first take a closer look at Ilich Ramírez Sánchez, alias Carlos Martínez Torres, the man behind the headlines. If anyone can be called the first international terrorist, it is this twenty-six-year-old [in 1976] Venezuelan, who speaks fluent Spanish, English, and Russian and passable French, Arabic, and German. Among his connections in the terror network were the Soviet KGB and the Cuban Dirección General de Inteligencia (DGI), an espionage agency completely controlled by the KGB. Besides working with various Palestinian and North African terrorist groups, Carlos established connections with the Japanese United Red Army; the Irish Republican Army; the last remnants of the Uruguayan Tupamaros and the South American terrorists; the Baader-Meinhof gang; the Eritrean Liberation Front; the Turkish Popular Liberation Front; Basque, Breton, and Corsican separatist movements; and, no doubt, others not yet discovered.

The French, who were the first to begin piecing together the Carlos jigsaw puzzle, were shocked by what they discovered. The unveiling of Carlos's Paris activities was described by Interior Minister Michel Poniatowski as "one of the most important cases of international terrorism to come to the attention of any Western police force in recent years." Considering what they had learned, it was a modest assessment even for the conservative French.

Carlos became an intriguing mystery. That old chestnut about one man's terrorist being another man's patriot was reroasted to a fine flavor in Third World countries. Even the right-wing daily *El Nacional* in Carlos's hometown of Caracas was comparing him to Simón Bolívar, the George Washington of South American independence. However, these questions remained: Who was Carlos and how serious was the threat of international terrorism? . . .

[Carlos's father] admired [Russian Communist revolutionary Vladimir Ilich] Lenin that he gave each of his three sons one of his hero's names—Ilich, born on October 12, 1949; Lenin, in 1951; and Vladimir, in 1958. However, his devotion to Lenin did not prevent him from amassing a fortune in real estate holdings. Nor did it stop him from providing his family with bourgeois comforts. From an early age, Ilich and his brothers traveled almost continuously with their mother around South America and the Caribbean. Accompanied by tutors, they studied the mores and languages of the countries visited—English in Jamaica and Miami, Portuguese in Brazil, and various dialects and customs in Mexico and Cuba.

At the age of fourteen, Ilich began his formal education at the Colegio Fermin Toro. That was in 1963, shortly after the dictator Marcos Pérez Jiménez was overthrown and the new liberal government of Rómulo Betancourt came under attack from the Right as well as from the Communist party, which had been banned for its support of anti-Betancourt guerrillas. Many of the students, including Ilich, demonstrated in support of the Communists.

Carlos Is Trained as a Revolutionary

Upon Ilich's graduation in 1966, Dr. Ramírez decided that his eldest son was ready to begin his political education. The school selected was Camp Mantanzas in Havana, Cuba, which specialized in political indoctrination and the art of subversion. The school, which was operated by Fidel Castro's secret service, was under the direction of the notorious Col. Victor Simonov, of the KGB, who became the operational boss of Cuba's DGI. The instructor in charge of guerrilla training was Antonio Dages Bouvier, an Ecuadorian, who would later share a London flat with Ilich.

One of the tactics taught for survival in the field encouraged the students to "get girls as helpers. Make friends with these seemingly harmless creatures for they are useful in providing refuge and in avoiding suspicion." This was one lesson that Ilich took to heart.

He studied for two years before his baptism of fire. His first mission was to land secretly on the Venezuelan coast and make contact. Something went wrong.

He was picked up almost immediately by the police. He was questioned and turned loose. He went back to Cuba only to return a few weeks later to help stir up student unrest at the University of Caracas. He fared no better. Picked up by the police, this time he was grilled for twelve hours and was not released until his father intervened.

Dr. Ramírez decided it was time for a change. Ilich had studied Russian in Cuba and now he was enrolled as a sociology student at the Patrice Lumumba University in Moscow, which is operated by the KGB as a training center for young revolutionaries from Third World nations. They are given an upper university education, along with political indoctrination. Promising students receive training in terrorism, sabotage, and guerrilla war techniques at camps in Odessa, Baku, Simferopol, and Tashkent [cities in the former Soviet Union]. Similar courses are provided for members of Moscow-controlled Communist parties, but in a separate program, through the Lenin Institute in Moscow, an appendage of the central committee of the Soviet party. Ilich received extensive training in firearms, explosives, the use of aliases, the forging of passports, clandestine communications, and safe houses.

There is no evidence that he objected to any of this. His father provided him with a generous allowance, enough to earn him quite a reputation as a "swinger." He loved poker, girls, music, conversation, good food, wine, and rum (not necessarily in that order) and was generous with his friends.

There is no available record of what actually happened in Moscow the two years Ilich was there. It is known that during the first year he was involved in an elaborately staged "spontaneous" demonstration outside of the Lebanese embassy, which had refused to renew the passports of its young nationals studying at Lumumba. He was seized for throwing a stone through a window, became involved in a scuffle with a Russian policeman, and was arrested.

The Playboy Revolutionary

At the start of his second year, he developed a stomach ulcer and went to join his mother in London, where he received treatment at a hospital for several months. His mother, who was then separated from his father, resided at the fashionable Phillimore Court, a five-story block in the heart of the Kensington shopping center. Señora Sánchez decorated her flat with beautiful antiques and objets d'art. These luxuries were made possible by a monthly allowance of $3,000 that she received from her estranged husband.

Captain Carlos Porras, naval attaché at the Venezuelan embassy in London, described Ilich's mother as "a charming and lovely woman who was invited to many social gatherings in London. Often all her three sons would come along with her. The last time I remember seeing Ilich was at a party in September or October of last year [1974]. He seemed to do nothing except travel a great deal. He was always coming back from somewhere or off to somewhere else. He gave the impression of a wealthy young man. He was always very fashionably dressed when I saw him.

"I don't think his mother knew what he was doing. I have a feeling he may have told her lies, but I can't say why. He and I said very little to each other—mostly just pleasantries. The last time we talked about his educational stay in Moscow. I didn't want to discuss politics with him, so I believe I changed the subject."

It is doubtful that anyone will ever really know what happened when Ilich returned to Moscow to complete his studies. It was reported that he spent so much time pursuing girls and bourgeois pleasures, habits his teachers characterized as debauchery, that he was expelled from the Soviet Union for "disrepute morals" and "provocative activities."

Needless to say, Western intelligence services were immediately alerted. Expulsion is an old trick used by the KGB to whitewash agents they plan on using in foreign countries. The machinations of the intelligence business being what they are, spies thrive on doublethink; and before long the thinking had come full circle, and Ilich was written off. With the benefit of hindsight, however, it is rather difficult, if not impossible, to believe that the Cubans and the Russians, who had Ilich under a microscope for nearly four years, could have failed to appreciate his potential.

Upon leaving the Soviet Union, Ilich traveled to East Berlin, where he was briefed on the leaders of the Baader-Meinhof gang, which had launched a terror campaign—bombings, murders, burnings, bank robberies—that years later West German chancellor Helmut Schmidt would call "the most serious challenge in the twenty-six-year history of our democracy."

Members of the Baader-Meinhof gang, as well as student terrorists, were constantly supported by the KGB-controlled East German secret police with houses in East Berlin, false papers and identity cards, money, arms and ammunition, and terrorist training. Transportation was provided from East Berlin to the Middle East, where they were placed in contact with the PFLP and other guerrilla groups. Among the first members of the Baader-Meinhof gang to receive guerrilla training at Palestinian camps were Andreas Baader, Ulrike Meinhof, Horst Mahler, Gudrun Ensslin, and Ingrid Siepmann.

When Ilich crossed over to West Berlin, he knew precisely whom to contact. The relationships he established on that first visit with Baader-Meinhof leaders were lasting ones. From there he traveled the "terror route" to Beirut, where he met Habash and his operational chief, Dr. Wadi Haddad, who was in charge of guerrilla training camps in Lebanon, Jordan, and South Yemen. This was Ilich's first involvement with the Palestinians, and it too would become a lasting one. Whatever credentials Ilich brought with him to Beirut, they were good enough to get him immediately into a leadership position. One of the significant contacts Ilich had made at Lumumba was his friendship with Mohammed Boudia, an Algerian classmate who became director of the PFLP's European network. It was an interesting relationship because they had a remarkable physical resemblance. This would later confuse Ha Mossad [the Israeli intelligence service] assassins who dogged Boudia's footsteps nearly two years before they got him—if they did.

Creating the Global Terror Network

Ha Mossad credits Boudia with initiating much of what they call the "global terror network." It also believes that Boudia served two functions in Europe: he recruited, organized, and designed many anti-Israeli actions for the PFLP, and as a KGB operative, he worked to unite various terrorist groups into an international network. His boss was Yuri Kotov, who was an expert in Middle East affairs and was listed as a Soviet foreign ministry attaché when he served as a KGB station officer in Israel. In 1967, with the break in diplomatic relations between the two countries, Kotov moved on to the Russian embassy in Beirut, where his reputation as a *bon vivant* followed him. Yet he made little effort to hide his true responsibilities.

Kotov followed Boudia to Paris, becoming chief of the KGB's Western European division. It was Kotov, Ha Mossad believes, who brought Ilich into the KGB structure. He contrived the expulsion from Lumumba as a smoke screen to confuse intelligence services.

It was not until February 1971 that Ilich returned to London, but instead of moving in with his mother and brothers, he shared two "safe" apartments with Bouvier, his old guerrilla training instructor from Camp Mantanzas. Middle-aged and of medium height, with short straight gray hair and a gray moustache, Bouvier, who wore horn-rimmed glasses and preferred conservative business suits, looked rather more like a banker than a terrorist. Although Ilich was receiving a monthly allowance of about $800 from his father, he had unlimited access to an account opened by Bouvier in his middle name, Dages.

As part of his cover, Ilich enrolled at the London School of Economics and joined his mother on the diplomatic cocktail circuit. To the people he met, he was just another wealthy Latin American playboy. Dressed in smartly tailored suits, with his beautiful mother on one arm and a lovely girl on the other, he cut quite a figure along Embassy Row. But that was his bourgeois front. A few embassy parties go a long way in establishing a young man's social credentials in a foreign capital. The impression he created was one of being bright and articulate, but seldom controversial. There were times when he expressed approval of the terrorist strategies of the Provisional Irish Republican Army (IRA). He would compare the Irish problem to that of the Palestinians, whose hostility toward Israel he supported. But that was as far as he would go, and then only in the heat of an argument others endorsed. What his wealthy acquaintances did not realize, of course, was that he was the liaison between the PFLP and the IRA, his first assignment in England.

Before long Ilich was frequenting the racially mixed Bayswater area, spending less time with his mother and on his studies, and more making friends with Latin

Americans, Basques, Africans, Arabs, and Japanese living in that polyglot ghetto. He met girls who were not as lovely as the ones he introduced to his mother but who were far more helpful in his work.

Ilich began making frequent flights to Europe and the Middle East, using a string of aliases and false passports to cover his tracks. Among the identities assumed were Cenon Clarke and Glenn Gebhard of New York; Adolfo José Muller Bernal of Chile; Carlos Andres Martínez Torres, a Peruvian economist; Hector Hugo DuPont, an Anglo-Frenchman; and Hector Hipodikon.

Ilich-Carlos met regularly with Boudia in Paris, and when Boudia was summoned to Beirut in May 1972 for a conference with Habash, Carlos was left in charge of the European operation. . . .

A Clandestine Terror War

During the fall and winter of 1972, following [Palestinian terrorist group] Black September's assault on the Olympic Village in Munich and the murder of eleven Israeli athletes, Mohammed Boudia became extremely jumpy. Ha Mossad assassination squads were sweeping across Europe methodically liquidating Arab terrorists. Wadal Adel Zwaiter, the Black September boss in Italy, was the first to be killed. Black September retaliated by murdering five Jordanian agents in West Germany suspected of passing information to the Israelis.

A clandestine war had been declared. Carlos's assignment was to kill Khader Kano, a Syrian journalist and double agent who was passing on information to the Israeli consulate in Belgium. Carlos followed him to a Paris apartment and pumped three bullets into his heart.

A Ha Mossad squad retaliated by killing Boudia's deputy, Dr. Mahmoud Hamshari, with a sophisticated explosive device. A powerful plastique bomb was planted under his telephone table, and to make sure they had the right man, the caller asked, "Is this really Dr. Hamshari?" "Lui-même," he replied. A split second later the bomb was triggered by a high-pitch tone transmitted on the line.

With Hamshari dead, Boudia appointed Carlos as his deputy. The tempo accelerated on both sides. There were a score of murders in Nicosia, Madrid, Khartoum, Rome, Beirut, and Paris. By June 28, 1973, Boudia's number had come up. He was blown up in his Renault sedan early one morning as he was leaving the Paris apartment of one of his many mistresses.

Not only was Carlos appointed by the PFLP to succeed Boudia (the assumption being that a Latin American was less likely to attract Ha Mossad's attention), but Kotov made him the KGB's European coordinator of terrorism. (The Russians are always anxious to demonstrate the weakness of democratic societies.) Yet Carlos remained a free agent and could initiate his own operations for the PFLP, or he could free-lance contract work for good revolutionaries like [Libyan leader Muammar] Qaddafi and [Algerian president Houari] Boumedienne.

Carlos Sets Up a Terrorist Unit

Carlos's first request to Habash was that he be permitted to revere Boudia's memory by setting up a special group of Arab commandos to be named after him. Habash agreed, but suggested that Carlos finance the Commando Boudia cell himself. For the necessary financing, Carlos turned to Qaddafi, who was already a staunch Black September supporter. Their main arms depot in Europe was located in the basement of the Libyan embassy in Bonn. As one terrorist observed, if someone had dropped a match in the place, half of the West German capital would have gone up in smoke.

It was at this time that Carlos began working with Michel Wahab Moukarbel, who was a Beirut interior decorator and Habash's paymaster and liaison in Europe. Posing as an art student at the Sorbonne, Moukarbel had a fetish for keeping meticulous records of all disbursements, however incriminating, incurred in the planning and execution of terrorist acts.

For his base of operation, Carlos selected a villa in Villiers sur Marne, just outside Paris, which was being used by a Turkish-Palestinian network. The place was equipped with a vast arsenal of weapons and explosives and a powerful radio set beamed on Beirut. As always, Carlos maintained his heavy traveling schedule, continuing his contacts with other terrorist groups and recruiting new members; in London and Paris, he stepped up his campaign of seducing Latin American girls who could provide him with safe houses.

Also during this period he was busy compiling an assassination list of public figures who were either Jewish or in sympathy with Israel. Some would receive letter bombs, but others, like J. Edward Sieff, who was honorary vice-president of the Zionist Federation of Great Britain, would merit a personal visit.

At seven o'clock on the evening of December 30, 1973, a hooded Carlos knocked at the door of Sieff's St. John's Wood [an area of London] home. When the butler answered, Carlos pointed his pistol and said, "I want to see Mr. Sieff." The terrified butler led Carlos to a bathroom on the first-floor landing and opened the door. Sieff, who was fully dressed, turned to face the two men, a surprised look on his face. Without a word, Carlos shot him in the mouth from a distance of about four feet. Sieff fell to the floor and Carlos ran from the house. Sieff miraculously survived because of remarkably strong teeth, which deflected the heavy 9-mm bullet to an angle that lodged it in his spine instead of his brain. Carlos was not linked with the shooting until the gun he used was found with other weapons and passports belonging to him.

Ted Kaczynski: The Unabomber

Kirkpatrick Sale

Theodore Kaczynski hated modern civilization, and blamed industry and technology for ruining the earth. Kaczynski himself tried to get away from the noise and pollution of modern society by moving to rural Montana, but felt such violations demanded a violent response.

Dubbed the Unabomber, the highly educated Kaczynski decided to take revenge on modern industry. He worked to develop explosives and techniques of delivering them to those he saw as responsible for wrecking the environment. Over seventeen years beginning in 1978, he orchestrated sixteen explosions, killing three people and injuring twenty-three. His targets ranged from students studying to be engineers to powerful heads of large corporations.

In 1995, Kaczynski sent a thirty-five-thousand-word treatise to the *New York Times* and the *Washington Post*. He demanded that the newspapers publish the document in its entirety or he would commit another bombing. The *Washington Post* published the article on September 19, 1995. Kaczynski's brother recognized the writing style and reported to the FBI that he suspected his brother was the Unabomber. Based on this information, Ted Kaczynski was arrested at his cabin in April 1996. He was sentenced to life in prison in 1998.

In the following selection, written prior to the publica-

Kirkpatrick Sale, "Is There a Method in His Madness?" *The Nation*, September 25, 1995. Copyright © 1995 by The Nation Magazine/The Nation Company, Inc. Reproduced by permission.

tion of Kaczynski's treatise, Kirkpatrick Sale argues that the treatise should be printed. Although he does not approve of Kaczynski's use of terror tactics, he contends that the Unabomber makes valid points about the harmful influence of technology on society. Sale is the author of *Rebels Against the Future: The Luddites and Their War on the Industrial Revolution*.

🐝   🐝   🐝

Any day now the powers at the *New York Times* and the *Washington Post* will have to decide whether they will print the full 35,000-word text of the document sent to them in late June 1995 by the man the Federal Bureau of Investigation is calling the Unabomber. In the letter that accompanied the text, he gave each paper three months to publish his screed, upon which he promises to "desist from terrorism," but he warned that if they refused he would "start building [his] next bomb." That deadline is September 29.

Publishing a Challenge to the "Industrial-Technological System"

Naturally the decision has been somewhat complicated for the two papers, since they don't want to seem to "give in to terrorist demands" and don't particularly like giving such publicity to the Unabomber's decidedly anti-establishmentarian opinions. They are especially perturbed by his demand to be allowed to publish additional 3,000-word pieces for the next three years to rebut any critics of the original, thus prolonging the Damoclean threat. And yet they obviously don't want to give the man an excuse to send out more of his mail bombs, two of which have killed and two wounded their recipients in the past three years.

I have read the full text of the Unabomber treatise—
the F.B.I. sent along two young female agents with
copies of it for me to peruse—and I would recommend
that either one of the papers publish it and trust the
man will keep his word about ending the mad, uncon-
scionable bombings. They should forget about the
"giving in to terrorism" excuse, which is mostly mean-
ingless in this case since there are no grand causes to be
satisfied, no hostages to be freed and no reason to think
that the threat would be repeated because it then becomes laughable. They needn't worry about the propaganda effect of printing it, since it is a woodenly written term paper, full of academic jargon and pop
psychology, repetitive and ill-argued, that will keep
only the most dedicated readers awake beyond its
opening paragraphs.

Which, I would say, is a shame. Because the central
point the Unabomber is trying to make—that "the
industrial-technological system" in which we live is a
social, psychological and environmental "disaster for
the human race"—is absolutely crucial for the American public to understand and ought to be on the fore-
front of the nation's political agenda. I say this, of
course, as a partisan. The Unabomber stands in a long
line of anti-technology critics where I myself have
stood, and his general arguments against industrial society and its consequences are quite similar to those I
have recently put forth in a book on the people who
might be said to have begun this tradition, the Luddites. Along with a number of people today [1995] who
might be called neo-Luddites—Jerry Mander, Chellis
Glendinning, Jeremy Rifkin, Bill McKibben, Wendell
Berry, Dave Foreman, Langdon Winner, Stephanie
Mills and John Zerzan among them—the Unabomber
and I share a great many views about the pernicious effect of the Industrial Revolution, the evils of modern

technologies, the stifling effect of mass society, the vast extent of suffering in a machine-dominated world and the inevitability of social and environmental catastrophe if the industrial system goes on unchecked.

We disagree, to be sure, about what is to be done about all this and the means by which to achieve it. In the course of his career, at least as the F.B.I. has reconstructed it, [since 1978] the Unabomber has carried out sixteen bombings, killing three people and injuring twenty-three others, apparently choosing targets in some way connected to modern technology—a technological institute at Northwestern University, the University of Utah business school, a Salt Lake City computer store, a University of California geneticist, and a Yale computer scientist, among others—to try to "propagate anti-industrial ideas and give encouragement to those who hate the industrial system." That strikes me as simple madness. Maiming and killing people does not normally propagate ideas, and in this case no one knew what ideas were in the Unabomber's mind until he started writing letters this past year and then delivered his treatise in June. As for getting the message across, the only message that anyone got for sixteen years was that some nut was attacking people associated with universities and computers (hence the F.B.I.'s tag, *Una*bomber).

But the bombings are going to get his document published, right or wrong, one way or another, and sooner rather than later. If the two newspapers don't publish it, *Penthouse* has offered to, and failing that, someone is sure to try to get it out as a pamphlet or send it over the Internet. That is what moves me to try to assess the treatise now, because I believe it would be a good idea to sort out its sound ideas from its errant ones, and to find the areas that ought not be discredited simply because of the agency that puts them forth—and as a service to all those who would fall asleep over the document itself.

Summarizing the Unabomber's Treatise

"Industrial Society and Its Future" is the modest-enough title, and it is labeled as "by FC," which the author describes as a "terrorist group" though there is no sign from the writing style here that more than one person is behind it, and the F.B.I. believes that the Unabomber is acting alone. (The fact that he has escaped detection for seventeen years—especially during this past year, when he has become the target of the largest manhunt in the agency's history—would tend to support that.) "FC" is variously cited as the initials for "Freedom Club" or "Freedom Collective," although it is popularly thought to stand for a vulgar comment about computers; it is not explained in his text.

The sixty-six pages that follow begin with two pages of trivial typo corrections, showing the kind of fastidiousness ("sovle" should be "solve:" "poit" should be "point") one might expect from a craftsman whose bombs the F.B.I. has described as "meticulously" constructed; then come fifty-six pages of argument divided into twenty-four subtitled sections and 232 numbered paragraphs; and it all ends with thirty-six footnotes, mostly qualifying statements in the text. That form, plus the leaden language and stilted diction, the fondness for sociological jargon and psychobabble, and the repeated use of "we argue that" and "we now discuss" and the like, make it certain that this was written by someone whose writing style, and probably whole intellectual development, was arrested in college.

The F.B.I. has said that it believes he was a student of the history of science, but on the evidence here he was a social psychology major with a minor in sociology, and he shows all the distressing hallmarks of the worst of that academic breed. He spends twelve pages, for example, on a strange and somewhat simplistic explanation of "something that we will call the power process," consisting of four elements "we call goal, effort and attainment of goal" plus "autonomy," all in an effort to explain why people today are unhappy and frustrated. Only someone trapped in the social sciences would talk that way.

Various professor types have been quoted in the papers saying how "bright" this fellow must be, but the arguments here are never very original and the line of reasoning is often quite convoluted. He has read a lot in certain areas—no poetry, though, I'll bet—and has thought a lot about the particular things that concern him, but aside from a few flashes there is no suggestion of anything more than a routine mind and a dutiful allegiance to some out-of-the-ordinary critics of modern society. I'm sure he makes good bombs, but grading him on his intellect I wouldn't give him more than a C+. I venture to say he didn't make it to his senior year.

The opus isn't helped by the fact that at least a third of it is essentially irrelevant, social-psych padding and scholarly back-and-forthing, one-hand-and-the-othering. Two long sections attacking "modern leftism" and "leftish" academics have nothing to do with his thesis, and I suspect they are offered because he had a bad time with certain sectarian groups in the early 1970s—no surprise—and with certain progress-minded, pro-technology Marxists he met in the academy.

Any good editor would have cut it.

But as near as I can fathom it after three careful readings, the Unabomber's argument would seem to be this:

• "Industrial-technological society" has succeeded to the point where, because of its size and complexity, it has constricted human freedom, meaning one's power to "control the circumstances of one's own life." Such freedoms as we do have are those permitted by the system consistent with its own ends—economic freedom to consume, press freedom to expose inefficiency and corruption—and do not in fact give individuals or groups true power, in the same sense that they have control over satisfying "life-and-death issues of one's existence: food, clothing, shelter and defense." "Today people live more by virtue of what the system does FOR them or TO them than by virtue of what they do for themselves. . . . Modern man is strapped down by a network of rules and regulations, and his fate depends on the actions of persons remote from him whose decisions he cannot influence."

• Industrial society *must* perform this way in order to succeed—"the system has to regulate human behavior closely in order to function"—and cannot be reformed to work differently. "Changes large enough to make a lasting difference in favor of freedom would not be initiated because it would be realized that they would gravely disrupt the system."

• Industrial society must increasingly work to constrict freedom and control behavior since "technology advances with great rapidity" and on many fronts: "crowding, rules and regulations, increasing dependence of individuals on large organizations, propaganda and other psychological techniques, genetic engineering, invasion of privacy through surveillance devices and computers, etc."

• But the problem of "control over human behavior" continues to bedevil this society, and right now "the system is currently engaged in a desperate struggle to overcome certain problems that threaten its survival," primarily social (the growing numbers of "rebels," "dropouts and resisters") but also economic and environmental. "If the system succeeds in acquiring sufficient control over human behavior quickly enough, it will probably survive. Otherwise it will break down. We think the issue will most likely be resolved within the next several decades, say 40 to 100 years."

• Therefore, the task of those who oppose the industrial system is to advance that breakdown by promoting "social stress and instability in industrial society," which presumably includes bombing, and by developing and propagating "an ideology that opposes technology," one that puts forth the "counter-ideal" of nature "in order to gain enthusiastic support." Thus, when the system becomes sufficiently stressed and unstable, a "revolution against technology may be possible."

A Barroom Critique of Society

Now, this is a reasonable enough argument—the Unabomber is not irrational, whatever else you can say about him—and I think it is even to some extent persuasive. There is nothing wild-eyed or rabble-rousing about it (it could actually use a lot more Paine-ist fomentation and furor) and the points are most often buttressed with careful arguments and examples—though nowhere, interestingly, a single statistic. It is too slow, too plodding, too repetitive; but you have to say its case is made in a competent, if labored, fashion. His critique of industrial society today is most telling, I think, and reads as if he'd spent a lot of time defending it in the back rooms of bars. . . . Just picking at random, I find these examples:

> The system does not and cannot exist to satisfy human needs. Instead, it is human behavior that has to be modified to fit the needs of the system. This has nothing to do with the political or social ideology that may pretend to guide the technological system. It is not the fault of capitalism and it is not the fault of socialism. It is the fault of technology, because the system is guided not by ideology but by technical necessity.

If the use of a new item of technology is INITIALLY
optional, it does not necessarily REMAIN optional,
because new technology tends to change society in
such a way that it becomes difficult or impossible for
an individual to function without using that technology. . . . Something like this seems to have happened
already with one of our society's most important psychological tools for enabling people to reduce (or at
least temporarily escape from) stress, namely, mass
entertainment. Our use of mass entertainment is
"optional" . . . yet mass entertainment is a means of
escape and stress-reduction on which most of us
have become dependent.

The technophiles are hopelessly naive (or self-
deceiving) in their understanding of social problems.
They are unaware of (or choose to ignore) the fact
that when large changes, even seemingly beneficial
ones, are introduced into a society, they lead to a
long sequence of other changes, most of which are
difficult to predict. . . . In fact, ever since the industrial revolution technology has been creating new
problems for society far more rapidly than it has
been solving old ones.

Not inspired, but thoughtful, perceptive enough,
when abstracted from its labored context.

What's surprising about all this, though, is that it
reads as if the Unabomber thinks he's the first person
who ever worked out such ideas. It is hard to believe,
but he seems woefully ignorant of the long Luddistic
strain in Western thought going back at least to
William Blake and Mary Shelley, and he does not once
cite any of the great modern critics of technology such
as Lewis Mumford, Jacques Ellul, Paul Goodman, Max
Weber, E.F. Schumacher or Rachel Carson, nor any of
the contemporary laborers in this vineyard. In one of his
letters to the *Times* he does say that "anyone who will
read the anarchist and radical environmentalist journals
will see that opposition to the industrial-technological

system is widespread and growing," so he must know something about the current critics, although he does not mention specific articles or authors or particular periodicals. (If I had to guess which has been most influential on him, I'd say the *Fifth Estate*, a feisty anti-technology paper published out of Detroit for the past thirty years, but he does not name it anywhere.)

That failure to ground himself in the Luddistic tradition, where both utopian and dystopian models proliferate, may be the reason that the Unabomber is so weak on envisioning the future, particularly the kind of revolution he seems to want.

I would agree with the Unabomber's general position that "to make a lasting change in the direction of development of any important aspect of a society, reform is insufficient," and I might even agree that in certain circumstances therefore "revolution is necessary." But I can't figure out at all what kind of revolution this is to be. He says that "a revolution does not necessarily involve an armed uprising or the overthrow of a government," a conviction he is so certain of he repeats it twice more, adding that "it may or may not involve physical violence," and in two footnotes he suggests that it might be "somewhat gradual or piecemeal" and might "consist only of a massive change of attitudes toward technology resulting in a relatively gradual and painless disintegration of the industrial system."

This is a somewhat peculiar position for a man who has been killing and injuring people in service to his dream of a new society, and I'm not sure what he thinks revolutions are or how they are achieved. If he has in mind something more like the Industrial Revolution or the Copernican revolution, he doesn't suggest how that might come about, and the sorts of strategies he ends up advocating—promoting social instability, destroying and wrecking "the system," seeing "its remnants . . .

smashed beyond repair"—sound an awful lot like a revolution with a good deal of violence. He even suggests at one point that the models are the French and Russian revolutions, both pretty bloody affairs.

The whole question of violence indeed is confused in the Unabomber's mind, oddly enough after seventeen years during which he must have been thinking about it a little. He never once addresses the reasons for his own string of bombings or explains what he thinks he has been accomplishing, other than to say that this was the way to have "some chance of making a lasting impression." He is critical of "leftists" who commit violence, because it is only "a form of 'liberation'" they justify "in terms of mainstream values . . . fighting against racism or the like," and later is critical of leftists because they are "against competition and against violence." His revolution is not necessarily to be violent, yet he never confronts the idea of a nonviolent revolution or how it would be strategically carried out.

The one task of revolutionaries the Unabomber is clear about is the business of producing an anti-technology "ideology," although he doesn't anywhere concern himself with the hard business of saying what that would consist of. But it doesn't much matter to him, since the primary purpose of this ideology is "to create a core of people who will be opposed to the industrial system on a rational, thought-out basis," an intellectual cadre who can then dish it out "in a simplified form" for the "unthinking majority" who "like to have such issues presented in simple, black-and-white terms." "History is made by active, determined minorities," you see, and "as for the majority, it will be enough to make them aware of the existence of the new ideology and remind them of it frequently." Lenin couldn't have put it better.

The Unabomber's idea of a systemic breakdown is, I

think, more plausible than his concept of revolution; one could see how, as the system was breaking down of its own weight and incompetence, unable to manage the problems its technology creates, this might be "helped along by revolutionaries." Just how the break-down would come about is not spelled out. The Un-abomber gives only a passing glance to the multiple en-vironmental disasters the system is producing for itself and never mentions the likelihood, as chaos theory pre-dicts, that the complex industrial house of cards will not hold. At least he does posit a "time of troubles" after which the human race would be "given a new chance."

A Vision Not Necessarily Inspired by Nature
I should note that the Unabomber, on the evidence here, does not have any special vision of an ecologically based future, as the newspapers have suggested. Indeed, he is no environmentalist, and I'd say he has only the faintest grasp of the principles of ecology. It's true that he refers to nature at one point—"That is, WILD na-ture!"—as a "positive ideal," but this is almost entirely cynical, nature as a concept that he figures will be use-ful in propaganda terms because it is "the opposite of technology," because "most people will agree that na-ture is beautiful" and because "in many people, nature inspires the kind of reverence that is associated with re-ligion." He shows no real understanding of the role of technology in enabling industrial society not only to exploit nature but to pass that off as legitimate, and not one individual environmental problem is addressed here, except overpopulation. . . .

It's clear enough that the Unabomber counts "radical environmentalists" as among those rightly opposing technology, and his use of wood in some of his bombs and his killing of a timber lobbyist in California suggests a further affinity. But he indicates no sympathy for the

kind of biocentric "deep ecology" and bioregionalism espoused by most of them, and his concerns are exclusively
anthropocentric, his appreciation of other species and
natural systems nil. He also mocks those who believe in
the "Gaia theory" of a living earth, common in many environmental groups: "Do its adherents REALLY believe
in it or are they just play-acting?"

In short, it feels to me that his appeal to nature is entirely utilitarian (like adding another little mechanism
to your bomb to make sure it works) rather than a
heartfelt passion, of which he seems to have very few in
any case. But if nature does not inspire his vision of the
future, it is hard to tell what does. Presumably he would
want, as a self-described anarchist, some kind of world
where "people live and work as INDIVIDUALS and
SMALL GROUPS," using "small-scale technology . . .
that can be used by small-scale communities without
outside assistance." But he nowhere bothers to hint at
how this future society would operate (other than to say
it would burn all technical books), nor does he refer to
any in the long line of anarcho-communal writers from
Peter Kropotkin to Murray Bookchin who have given a
great deal of thought to the configurations of just such
a society.

It's true that the Unabomber offers the defense at one
point that "a new kind of society cannot be designed on
paper" and when revolutionaries or utopians set up a
new kind of society, it never works out as planned."
That gives him leeway to avoid discussing what kind of
world he wants (even in a three-page section called
"THE FUTURE"); unfortunately, it also leaves a gap-
ing hole in his treatise. Even those who agree that the
industrial system should be torn down will want to get
some idea of what is supposed to replace it before they
are moved to endorse the cause, much less become the
revolutionaries the Unabomber wants.

A "Crucial Message" Delivered by a Terrorist

So, in sum, what are we to make of this strange document? So important to its author that he is prepared to kill people (even though he has written that he is "getting tired of making bombs") to get it published in a major newspaper. So embarrassing to those newspapers that they don't know what to do with it.

It is the statement of a rational and serious man, deeply committed to his cause, who has given a great deal of thought to his work and a great deal of time to this expression of it. He is prescient and clear about the nature of the society we live in, what its purposes and methods are, and how it uses its array of technologies to serve them; he understands the misery and anxiety and constriction this creates for the individual and the wider dangers it poses for society and the earth. He truly believes that a campaign of social disorder led by misfits, rebels, dropouts and saboteurs (and presumably terrorists), coupled with the concerted propaganda work of a dedicated intellectual elite, has a chance to cause or hasten the breakdown of industrial society, and this motivates him in his grisly work.

The document is also the product of a limited and tunnel-visioned man, with a careful and dogged but somewhat incoherent mind, filled with a catalogue of longstanding prejudices and hatreds, academically trained, occasionally inventive, purposeful and humorless. He is amoral, not to say cold-blooded, about acts of terrorism, which are regarded as an effective tactic in service to the larger cause. He is convinced enough in his cause to have produced this long justification for it, complete with numerous bold assertions and his own "principles of history," but he repeatedly finds qualifications and reservations and indeed ends up calling the article no more "than a crude approximation to the truth," as if to suggest that somewhere within he is not quite confident.

All in all, I think despite its flaws it is a document worth publishing, and not only because that could presumably help stop the killing. There is a crucial message at the core of it for those with fortitude enough to get through it, and unless that message is somehow heeded and acted on we are truly a doomed society hurtling toward a catastrophic breakdown. I can't expect the *Times* and the *Post* to give much credence to that idea—and they can lard it with their own dissents and denials if they choose—but they might just realize that there is a growing body of people these days beginning at last to understand the increasing perils of the technosphere we have created. For, as the *New Yorker* recently put it, there's a little of the Unabomber in all of us.

Timothy McVeigh Bombs the Oklahoma City Federal Building

Ted Ottley

To most observers Timothy McVeigh was an ordinary American. Born in 1968, he seemed to be a happy child. He graduated from high school, worked at Burger King, and eventually joined the army. At some point along the way he developed ideas that led him to commit a major terrorist act, the bombing of the Alfred P. Murrah Federal Building in Oklahoma City.

In the following selection, journalist Ted Ottley describes McVeigh's road to terrorism. Soon after graduating from high school, McVeigh was influenced by a novel written by a neo-Nazi. He became obsessed with guns and survivalism. McVeigh joined the army because he enjoyed working with weapons. He fought in the 1991 Gulf War, but when he failed to become a Special Forces soldier, he quit the army. Disillusioned, he drifted around the country, selling guns at gun shows. Eventually he met up with old army friends who planned and carried out what was until the September 11, 2001, attacks the worst terrorist incident on American soil. McVeigh was convicted of carrying out

Ted Ottley, "The Timothy McVeigh Story: The Oklahoma Bomber," www. crimelibrary.com, 2003. Copyright © 2003 by Courtroom Television Network, LLC. Reproduced by permission.

the attack in 1997 and sentenced to death. He was executed in June 2001.

Ted Ottley is a journalist and writer. He has written for publications in England, Australia, and the United States. He has also written a series of mystery novels for teenagers. In addition to writing, he has operated a recording studio and managed a dude ranch.

🐝   🐝   🐝

It was April 19, 1995, a perfect, sun-drenched Oklahoma morning in springtime. Against a perfect blue-sky background, a yellow Ryder Rental truck carefully made its way through the streets of downtown Oklahoma City.

Just after 9 A.M., the vehicle pulled into a parking area outside the Alfred P. Murrah Building and the driver stepped down from the truck's cab and casually walked away. A few minutes later, at 9:02, all hell broke loose as the truck's deadly 4000-pound cargo blasted the government building with enough force to shatter one third of the seven-story structure to bits.

Glass, concrete, and steel rained down. Indiscriminately mixed in the smoldering rubble were adults and children alive and dead.

The perpetrator twenty-seven-year-old Timothy James McVeigh by now safely away from the devastation was convinced he acted to defend the Constitution, for he saw himself as crusader, warrior avenger and *hero*.

But in reality, he was little more than a misguided coward. He never even heard clearly the sound of the initial sirens of emergency vehicles rushing to the scene. Because, blocks away, he was wearing earplugs to protect himself from the roar of a blast so powerful it lifted pedestrians off the ground. . . .

Childhood

As a child, Timothy McVeigh was full of fun and easy to like. Born April 23, 1968, he was the middle child of three, and the only boy. He grew up in Pendleton, NY, a small town just south of the Canadian border by the Erie Canal. Mainly white, blue collar and Christian, it was the kind of place where kids could run into a neighbor's house without knocking. Young "Timmy" did just that, and was always welcome.

The town, established by Sylvester Pendleton Clark, was called after his mother's maiden name. It maintains a strong connection with nearby Lockport famous before the Civil War as a departure point for slaves escaping to Canada and freedom. Clark himself was a rugged individual who had led a rebellion against government taxes in the early 1800s. A strong independent spirit still characterizes Pendleton.

Tim's father, Bill McVeigh, worked mainly in a local car radiator plant, but it was his grandfather Eddie McVeigh who influenced the boy most. He taught young Tim about the outdoors, hunting and, significantly, introduced him to guns. . . .

When he was nine years old, a crippling blizzard hit town. Out for drinks at a local hotel, his mother phoned to say they were snowbound, and that she wouldn't make it home that night. It was a blizzard where people froze to death, were buried in cars and generally trapped. By the time it let up, days had passed and many had run out of basic supplies. As Tim helped shovel neighbors' roadways, he learned about survival. The family began stockpiling food, water and other necessities to cope with the enemy weather.

McVeigh Fascinated by Guns

At age thirteen, his Grandpa Eddie presented Tim with a .22 caliber rifle. It was the first of many guns he would own. He was so into firearms that he answered the question "What do you want to be when you grow up?" with "gun shop owner." Furthermore, he used to take one of his guns to school sometimes to impress the other guys. It worked.

At home, the family experienced continued turbulence. His mother, Mickey liked to socialize and stay out late. She was torn between fun and family. Finally, when Tim was in his teens, she left for good and in 1986 she and Bill finally divorced. It was the same year Tim graduated from high school with honors. . . .

On graduating, Tim quit his high school job at Burger King, sold his Commodore 64 computer and spent much of his time researching the Second Amendment. He was developing an intense interest in the rights of gun owners. At his father's insistence, he did a stint at business college, but found it too monotonous. His days of formal education were over.

It was at this time that he discovered *The Turner Diaries*. He obsessed over this novel by former American Nazi Party official William Pierce. Writing under the name Andrew Macdonald, Pierce pumps out a litany of hate through the main character Earl Turner. This "hero" demonstrates his contempt for gun control laws by truck-bombing the Washington FBI headquarters. He also appears to favor Adolf Hitler and dismiss blacks and Jews as worthy of annihilation.

About the same time, the movie *Red Dawn* [about a Russian invasion of the United States] helped convince McVeigh it was time to become a survivalist like Jedd the film's hero played by Patrick Swayze. In the movie, Jedd leads his band of followers into the woods with seemingly endless rounds of ammo and supplies they'll need to survive. Their mission is to destroy an invading Communist army.

Because McVeigh needed funds to finance his growing fantasies, he went back to work for Burger King while he looked for a better paying job. Soon he was employed as an armed security guard with the Burke Armored Car Service, where he's remembered as a diligent employee.

By now, he was twenty years old. He had a uniform, a gun and an armored vehicle to drive around in. But he longed for better targets, bigger guns and real tanks.

So, on May 24, 1988, Tim McVeigh joined the Army. There, he'd meet two men who would join him on his trip to terrorism.

McVeigh had finally found his calling. The Army was everything he wanted in life, and more. When he joined, he was no leader, but an eager follower. There was discipline, a sense of order, and all the training a man could want in survivalist techniques. Most of all, there was an endless supply of weapons, and instruction on how to use and maintain them.

The tough basic training at Fort Benning, Georgia, saw him determined to excel if he did, he could earn entrance into the Army's elite Special Forces club. His sights were set on the Green Beret. Had he stayed focused, he likely would have made it.

But fate derailed his ambitions in many ways.

Army Buddies

In basic training, he met two other soldiers who were to support his obsessive journey into crime: Terry Lynn Nichols and Michael Fortier.

For the Army, Terry Nichols joined up at a relatively mature age. Called "the old man" by the other recruits, he was twelve years older than McVeigh. They connected on the rifle range at Fort Benning and quickly formed a bond. Initially, McVeigh looked up to Nichols, but the balance shifted as their friendship grew. Nichols, who was married with a son did not warm to the strict

Army regimen, although he liked the weaponry. He had joined only because his other attempts at holding down a job had failed. He didn't last, finally taking a hardship discharge after his wife had left him he felt required to go home to raise his son.

Fortier, like McVeigh, was young, and his profile very different. He was a pill-popping, pot-smoking man who probably signed up because of his family's military background. Fortier and McVeigh became closer after Nichols had opted out of the service.

The three went from basic training to Fort Riley, Kansas. There, McVeigh became a gunner on the Bradley fighting vehicle. He'd already excelled in marksmanship and he exhibited an unusually high level of skill with every weapon he encountered. As a result, he quickly advanced and was remembered as "an excellent soldier."

His military prowess earned him an invitation to try out for the Special Forces and he trained hard on his own time to ensure his chance to wear the Green Beret. But before he was due to be evaluated, Saddam Hussein cast a shadow over his plans.

In 1991, the Gulf War erupted and McVeigh's First Infantry Division was dispatched to the Persian Gulf to serve in Desert Storm. Again, McVeigh excelled as a soldier and served with distinction. He became lead gunner on the Bradley fighting vehicle in the first platoon. In the Army, Tim had become a VIP.

When he returned home, he'd earned a fistful of decorations including the coveted Bronze Star.

Now, he renewed his attempt to gain acceptance into the Special Forces. But against advice to wait until he built up the stamina lost in Desert Storm, he tried out anyway. He was simply not fit enough to cut it. This failure triggered a waning interest in military life and he quit the Army. . . .

He decided to seek out his old Army buddies. He wanted to spend some time with Michael Fortier in Kingman, Arizona, then visit Michigan to see Terry Nichols now staying on a farm owned by his brother James Nichols. With the prospect of Fortier and Nichols back in his life, McVeigh felt like he could belong again. They were kindred spirits who welcomed his anti-government rhetoric.

The Waco Incident

One of the events that triggered his final drastic act had begun on February 28, 1993, when federal agents raided the property of the religious group called the Branch Davidians, headed by the charismatic David Koresh. When the ATF (Alcohol, Tobacco and Firearms) agents charged the Branch Davidian compound, lives were lost and many wounded. The Branch Davidians held their ground and the standoff continued.

Sensing that the rights of the group to bear arms were being violated, McVeigh headed for Waco to lend support and make a few bucks at the same time. He stocked up on items he could hand out or sell including anti-government leaflets and bumper stickers bearing messages like "Politicians Love Gun Control," "Fear the Government That Fears Your Gun," "A Man with a Gun Is a Citizen, a Man Without a Gun Is a Subject." When he arrived, he wanted to see the compound where the standoff was continuing, but agents blocked his way. When he returned to an area where he could park and distribute his wares, student reporter Michelle Rauch talked McVeigh into an interview.

He told Rauch, "The government is afraid of the guns people have because they have to have control of the people at all times. Once you take away the guns, you can do anything to the people," and "The government is continually growing bigger and more powerful, and the people need to prepare to defend themselves against government control."

He left Waco a few days later and went to stay with Michael Fortier and his wife Lori in their mobile home in Kingman. But although he and Fortier were indeed soul mates when it came to politics, Fortier's drug habits bored McVeigh to the point where he soon moved on to Tulsa, Oklahoma, and Wanenmacher's World's largest Gun and Knife Show just one of many gun shows he visited on his travels.

These events buoyed McVeigh's spirits tremendously. Gun show people thought the way he did. One in particular Roger Moore had invited McVeigh to visit his Arkansas ranch. Moore often went by the name "Bob Miller" at the shows. He didn't want people to know too much about him. When McVeigh arrived at the Moore ranch, he understood why. When Moore showed McVeigh around, it was obvious the place was loaded with weapons, explosive materials and other valuables. And security was almost non-existent. Moore would live to regret McVeigh's visit. As would Terry Nichols, whose home was Tim's next port of call.

McVeigh Outraged by Government Attack

When McVeigh arrived at the Nichols' Decker, Michigan, farm, the reports coming out of Waco dominated the airwaves. In between watching the standoff on TV, the Nichols brothers introduced Tim to the art of making explosives out of readily available materials. Tim was interested, but not yet ready to act on the information. Then, on April 19, 1993, they watched in horror as the Branch Davidians' compound was battered and burned into oblivion.

This so outraged McVeigh and Nichols that they decided someone had to stop the ATF. *Someone* would have to make a stand.

Like the heroes in *Red Dawn*.

Like the hero in *The Turner Diaries*. . . .

On September 13, 1994, the gun shows McVeigh attended had become somber occasions. New laws had been passed to stop the manufacture of many types of weaponry, including a range of semi-automatic rifles and handguns. Gun traders and buyers alike were outraged to learn the government was controlling their "right to bear arms."

To McVeigh, it also meant his livelihood was endangered. He had been buying weapons under his own name and charging a brokerage fee to other buyers those who didn't want their names on government forms.

Planning the Attack

Paranoia rose on rumors that owners would be subject to surprise searches of their homes and businesses. McVeigh decided that action could no longer be postponed. From the Nichols home in Marion, Kansas, he wrote Fortier. He insisted the time had come for action, and he wanted Fortier to join him and Terry Nichols in their protest. Imitating *The Turner Diaries*, they planned to blow up a federal building. McVeigh cautioned Fortier against telling his wife, Lori, an instruction Fortier ignored.

Furthermore, Fortier said he would never be part of the plan "not unless there was a U.N. tank in my front yard!"

Undeterred, McVeigh and Nichols took advice from various bomb-building manuals. They followed the recipe and stockpiled their materials bought under the alias Mike Havens in rented storage sheds. The recipe also called for other ingredients like blasting caps and liquid nitro methane, which they stole. But that's not all they stole.

To pay for their despicable enterprise, Nichols robbed gun collector Roger Moore at gunpoint. Moore claimed the thief had taken a variety of guns, gold, silver and jewels about sixty thousand dollars' worth. Nichols also stole Moore's van to haul away the loot. When police made a list of visitors to the ranch, McVeigh's name was on it. . . .

In mid-December 1994, McVeigh and the Fortiers met in McVeigh's room at the Mojave Motel in Kingman, Arizona. There, he had Lori gift wrap boxes containing blasting caps in Christmas paper. He then promised Fortier a cache of weapons from the Moore robbery if he would accompany McVeigh back to Kansas. On the way, McVeigh drove through Oklahoma City to show Fortier the building he intended to bomb, and the route he would take to walk away from the building before the blast. They parted.

The getaway car would be his 1977 yellow Marquis since his other car had been damaged in an accident. The plan was for Nichols to follow the car in his truck. After McVeigh parked it away from the bombsite, they would drive back to Kansas. The night before the bombing, they left the Marquis after McVeigh removed the license plate and left a note on it saying it needed a battery. Then, they drove away and Nichols dropped him off at his motel.

The next afternoon, McVeigh picked up the Ryder truck and parked it at the Dreamland Motel for the night. The following morning he drove it to the Herington storage unit. When Nichols finally arrived late they piled the bomb components in the truck and drove to Geary Lake to mix the bomb. When they were done, Nichols went home and McVeigh stayed with the lethal Ryder vehicle.

The Blood of Patriots and Tyrants

He parked in a gravel lot for the night and waited for the dawn and the drive to his target. He was dressed for the mission in his favorite T-shirt. On the front was a picture of Abraham Lincoln with the motto "sic semper tyrannis," the words Booth shouted before he shot Lincoln. The translation: Thus ever to tyrants.

On the back of the T-shirt was a tree with blood dripping from the branches. It read, "The tree of liberty must be refreshed from time to time with the blood of patriots and tyrants."

Like his role model in *The Turner Diaries*, he headed for a federal building where he was convinced ATF agents were working. There, the people of Oklahoma City would pay a terrible price for McVeigh's compulsive and irrational paranoia.

Appendix of Documents

Document 1: Terror Is Necessary to Preserve the Revolution

Anaxagoras Chaumette, the mayor of Paris and a supporter of Maximilien Robespierre, declares in 1793 that the situation in the city and the country is becoming intolerable because of those who are using the revolution for their own ends. He demands an army be formed to destroy the internal enemies of the revolution.

Citizen legislators, the citizens of Paris are tired of a situation that has been uncertain and wavering for too long and want to settle their fate once and for all. Europe's tyrants, along with the state's internal enemies, persist outrageously in their hideous plot to starve the French People into submission and to force them to shamefully trade their liberty and sovereignty for a piece of bread—something they will certainly never do.

New lords, just as cruel, just as greedy, and just as brazen as those they replaced, have risen up in the ruins of feudalism. They have leased or bought the properties of their former masters and continue to follow the well-worn paths of crime, to profit from public misery, to stem the tide of abundance, and to tyrannize those who destroyed tyranny. . . .

Every day we learn of new betrayals and new crimes. Every day we become upset at the discovery and the reappearance of new conspiracies. Every day new disturbances stir up the Republic, ready to drag it into their stormy whirlwinds, hurling it into the bottomless abyss of the centuries to come. But where is that powerful being whose terrible cry will reawaken sleeping justice—or rather justice that has been paralyzed, dazed by the clamor of factions—and force it at last to strike off criminal heads? Where is that powerful being who will crush all these reptiles who corrupt everything they touch and whose venomous stings stir up our citizens, transforming political gatherings into gladiatorial arenas where each passion, each interest, finds apologists and armies?

Legislators, it is time to put an end to the impious struggle that has been going on since 1789 between the sons and daughters of the nation and those who have abandoned it. Your fate, and ours, is tied to the unvarying establishment of the republic. We must either destroy its enemies, or they will destroy us. They have thrown down the gauntlet in the midst of the People, who have picked it up. They have stirred up agitation. They have attempted to separate, to divide the mass of the citizens, in order to crush the People and to avoid being crushed themselves. Today, the mass of the People, who are without resources, must destroy them using their own weight and willpower. . . .

We are charged with demanding the creation of the revolutionary army which you have already decreed but which the guilty, through plotting and fear, have aborted. [Unanimous applause breaks out several times.] Let this army form its core in Paris immediately, and from every department through which it passes, let all men join who want a republic united and indivisible. Let an incorruptible and formidable tribunal follow this army, as well as that deadly tool which, with a single stroke, ends both the conspiracies and the days of their authors. Let this tribunal be tasked with making avarice and cupidity cough up the wealth of the land, that inexhaustible wet nurse of all children. Let it bear the following words on its standards, which shall be its constant order: *Peace to men of good will; war on those who would starve people; protection for the weak; war on tyrants; justice; and no oppression.*

Finally, let this army be established such that there remains in each city sufficient forces to restrain malicious people.

Anaxagoras Chaumette, mayor of Paris, speech to the French National Convention, September 5, 1793.

Document 2: Hitler Justifies Brutality and Terror

In the following speech, given ten days before the Nazi invasion of Poland that began World War II, Adolf Hitler justifies brutality and terror as necessary tactics.

Our strength lies in our quickness and in our brutality; Genghis Khan has sent millions of women and children into death knowingly and with a light heart. History sees in him only the great founder of States. As to what the weak Western European civilisation asserts about me, that is of no account. I have given the command and I shall shoot everyone who utters one word of criticism, for the goal to be obtained in the war is not that of reaching certain lines but of physically demolishing the opponent. And so for the present only in the East I have put my death-head formations in place with the command relentlessly and without compassion to send into death many women and children of Polish origin and language. Only thus we can gain the living space [*lebensraum*] that we need. . . .

Be hard, be without mercy, act more quickly and brutally than the others. The citizens of Western Europe must tremble with horror. That is the most human way of conducting a war. For it scares the others off.

Adolf Hitler, speech delivered at Obersalzberg, Germany, on August 22, 1939.

Document 3: The Irgun Proclaims the Revolt in Palestine

Menachem Begin's Irgun launched a guerrilla war against the British forces occupying Palestine in early 1944. It also began armed violence against the Palestinian Arabs of the territory. The following is the text of a poster proclaiming the start of the revolt that appeared on the streets of the Jewish community on February 1, 1944.

TO THE HEBREW NATION IN ZION!

We are in the last stage of the world war. Each and every nation is now conducting its national reckoning. What are its triumphs and what were its losses? What road must it take in order to achieve its goal and fulfil its mission? Who are its friends and who its enemies? Who is the true ally and who the traitor? And who is proceeding towards the decisive battle? . . .

Sons of Israel, Hebrew youth!

We stand at the final stage of the war, we face an historic decision on our future destiny. The truce proclaimed when war broke out has been violated by the British authorities. The rulers of the country have taken into account neither loyalty nor concessions nor sacrifice; they have continued to implement their aim: the liquidation of sovereign Zionism. . . .

We must draw the necessary conclusions without wavering. There can no longer be a truce between the Hebrew nation and youth and the British administration of Eretz Israel, which is betraying our brethren to Hitler. Our nation will fight this regime, fight to the end. . . .

Our fighting youth will not be deterred by victims, blood and suffering. They will not surrender, will not rest until they restore our past glory, until they ensure our people of a homeland, freedom, honor, bread, justice and law. And if you help them, then your own eyes will soon behold the return to Zion and the rebirth of Israel. May God be with us and aid us!

Anonymous, "To the Hebrew Nation in Zion," poster appearing in Palestine, February 1, 1944.

Document 4: Mao Zedong Institutes the People's Dictatorship

In a speech to the Chinese Communist Party shortly after achieving power in China in 1949, Mao Zedong lays out the future of his revolution. He says that dictatorial powers are necessary in order to establish Communist society and combat imperialism. He warns would-be "reactionaries"—those classes who oppose the revolution—that they will be "remoulded."

"You are dictatorial." My dear sirs, you are right, that is just what we are. All the experience the Chinese people have accumulated through several decades teaches us to enforce the people's democratic dictatorship, that is, to deprive the reactionaries of the right to speak and let the people alone have that right.

"Who are the people?" At the present stage in China, they are the working class, the peasantry, the urban petty bourgeoisie and the national bourgeoisie. These classes, led by the working class and the Communist Party unite to form their own state and elect their own government they enforce their dictatorship over the running dogs of imperialism—the landlord class and bureaucrat-bourgeoisie, as well as the representatives of those classes, the Kuomintang reactionaries and their accomplices—suppress them, allow them only to behave themselves and not to be unruly in word or deed. If they speak or act in an unruly way, they will be promptly stopped and punished. Democracy is practised within the ranks of the people, who enjoy the rights of freedom of speech, assembly, association and so on. The right to vote belongs only to the people, not to the reactionaries. The combination of these two aspects, democracy for the people and dictatorship over the reactionaries, is the people's democratic dictatorship. . . .

The state apparatus, including the army, the police and the courts, is the instrument by which one class oppresses another. It is an instrument for the oppression of antagonistic classes; it is violence and not "benevolence". "You are not benevolent!" Quite so. We definitely do not apply a policy of benevolence to the reactionaries and towards the reactionary activities of the reactionary classes. Our policy of benevolence is applied only within the ranks of the people, not beyond them to the reactionaries or to the reactionary activities of reactionary classes. . . .

Here, the method we employ is democratic, the method of persuasion, not of compulsion. When anyone among the people breaks the law, he too should be punished, imprisoned or even sentenced to death; but this is a matter of a few individual cases, and it differs in principle from the dictatorship exercised over the reactionaries as a class.

As for the members of the reactionary classes and individual reactionaries, so long as they do not rebel, sabotage or create trouble after their political power has been overthrown, land and work will be given to them as well in order to allow them to live and remould themselves through labour into new people. If they are not willing to work, the people's state will compel them to work. . . .

Mao Zedong, speech to commemorate the twenty-eighth anniversary of the Communist Party of China, Beijing, China, June 30, 1949.

Document 5: Stalin's Successor Denounces the Dictator's Cult of Personality

The following selection is part of a secret speech delivered by Communist Party secretary Nikita Khrushchev at the Communist Party Congress of the Soviet Union, February 25, 1956. In it, Khrushchev contrasts the reasonable leadership of the first Soviet Communist leader, Vladimir Ilich Lenin, with Joseph Stalin's brutal repression.

Stalin originated the concept "enemy of the people." This term automatically made it unnecessary that the ideological errors of a man or men engaged in a controversy be proven. It made possible the use of the cruelest repression, violating all norms of revolutionary legality, against anyone who in any way disagreed with Stalin, against those who were only suspected of hostile intent, against those who had bad reputations. The concept "enemy of the people" actually eliminated the possibility of any kind of ideological fight or the making of one's views known on this or that issue, even [issues] of a practical nature. On the whole, the only proof of guilt actually used, against all norms of current legal science, was the "confession" of the accused himself. As subsequent probing has proven, "confessions" were acquired through physical pressures against the accused. This led to glaring violations of revolutionary legality and to the fact that many entirely innocent individuals—[persons] who in the past had defended the Party line—became victims.

We must assert that, in regard to those persons who in their time had opposed the Party line, there were often no sufficiently serious reasons for their physical annihilation. The formula "enemy of the people" was specifically introduced for the purpose of physically annihilating such individuals. . . .

Everyone knows how irreconcilable Lenin was with the ideological enemies of Marxism, with those who deviated from the correct Party line. At the same time, however, Lenin, as is evident from the given document, in his practice of directing the Party demanded the most intimate Party contact with people who had shown indecision or temporary nonconformity with the Party line, but whom it was possible to return to the Party path. Lenin advised that such people should be patiently educated without the application of extreme methods.

Lenin's wisdom in dealing with people was evident in his work with cadres.

An entirely different relationship with people characterized Stalin. Lenin's traits—patient work with people, stubborn and painstaking education of them, the ability to induce people to follow him without using compulsion, but rather through the ideological influence on them of the whole collective—were entirely foreign to Stalin. He discarded the Leninist method of convincing and educating, he abandoned the method of ideological struggle for that of administrative violence, mass repressions and terror. He acted on an increasingly larger scale and more stubbornly through punitive organs, at the same time often violating all existing norms of morality and of Soviet laws.

Arbitrary behavior by one person encouraged and permitted arbitrariness in others. Mass arrests and deportations of many thousands of people, execution without trial and without normal investigation created conditions of insecurity, fear and even desperation.

This, of course, did not contribute toward unity of the Party ranks and of all strata of working people, but, on the contrary, brought about annihilation and the expulsion from the Party of workers who were loyal but inconvenient to Stalin.

Nikita Khrushchev, secret speech to the Twentieth Congress of the Communist Party of the Soviet Union, February 25, 1956.

Document 6: The Palestinian National Charter Endorses Armed Struggle Against Israel

The following excerpt from the 1968 Palestinian National Convenant commits the Palestinian National Convention to "armed struggle"—meaning guerrilla tactics and terrorism—against the Israelis.

Palestine is the homeland of the Arab Palestinian people; it is an indivisible part of the Arab homeland, and the Palestinian people are an integral part of the Arab nation. . . .

It is a national duty to bring up individual Palestinians in an Arab revolutionary manner. All means of information and education must be adopted in order to acquaint the Palestinian with his country in the most profound manner, both spiritual and material, that is possible. He must be prepared for the armed struggle and ready to sacrifice his wealth and his life in order to win back his homeland and bring about its liberation. . . .

The phase in their history, through which the Palestinian people are now living, is that of national (watani) struggle for the liberation of Palestine. Thus the conflicts among the Palestinian national forces are secondary, and should be ended for the sake of the basic conflict that exists between the forces of Zionism and of imperialism on the one hand, and the Palestinian Arab people on the other. On this basis the Palestinian masses, regardless of whether they are residing in the national homeland or in diaspora (mahajir) constitute—both their organizations and the individuals—one national front working for the retrieval of Palestine and its liberation through armed struggle. . . .

Armed struggle is the only way to liberate Palestine. This it is the overall strategy, not merely a tactical phase. The Palestinian Arab people assert their absolute determination and firm resolution to continue their armed struggle and to work for an armed popular revolution for the liberation of their country and their return to it. They also assert their right to normal life in Palestine and to exercise their right to self-determination and sovereignty over it. . . .

Commando action constitutes the nucleus of the Palestinian popular liberation war. This requires its escalation, comprehensiveness, and the mobilization of all the Palestinian popular and educational efforts and their organization and involvement in the armed Palestinian revolution.

Palestinian National Charter: Resolutions of the Palestine National Council, Cairo, Egypt, July 1–17, 1968.

Document 7: The Unabomber, Theodore Kaczynski, Advocates Revolution Against Industrial Society

In September 1995 the so-called Unabomber's manifesto was printed in the Washington Post *as an eight-page supplement. Theodore Kaczynski had agreed to stop the bombings if either the* New York Times *or the* Post *agreed to print his work. Below is the introduction to the manifesto, which lays out Kaczynski's case against industrial society and the need to revolutionize modern life.*

1. The Industrial Revolution and its consequences have been a disaster for the human race. They have greatly increased the life-expectancy of those of us who live in "advanced" countries, but they have destabilized society, have made life unfulfilling, have subjected human beings to indignities, have led to widespread psychological suffering (in the Third World to physical suffering as well) and have inflicted severe damage on the natural world. The continued development of technology will worsen the situation. It will certainly subject human beings to greater indignities and inflict greater damage on the natural world, it will probably lead to greater social disruption and psychological suffering, and it may lead to increased physical suffering even in "advanced" countries.

2. The industrial-technological system may survive or it may break down. If it survives, it MAY eventually achieve a low level of physical and psychological suffering, but only after passing through a long and very painful period of adjustment and only at the cost of permanently reducing human beings and many other living organisms to engineered products and mere cogs in the social machine. Furthermore, if the system survives, the consequences will be inevitable: There is no way of reforming or modifying the system so as to prevent it from depriving people of dignity and autonomy.

3. If the system breaks down the consequences will still be very painful. But the bigger the system grows the more disastrous the results of its breakdown will be, so if it is to break down it had best break down sooner rather than later.

4. We therefore advocate a revolution against the industrial system. This revolution may or may not make use of vi-

olence: it may be sudden or it may be a relatively gradual process spanning a few decades. We can't predict any of that. But we do outline in a very general way the measures that those who hate the industrial system should take in order to prepare the way for a revolution against that form of society. This is not to be a POLITICAL revolution. Its object will be to overthrow not governments but the economic and technological basis of the present society.

Theodore Kaczynski, "Unabomber Manifesto," *Washington Post*, September 1995.

Document 8: Seeking Justice in Cambodia

In the following excerpt, the head of the U.S. Senate Judiciary Committee, Patrick Leahy, reflects on the 1998 death of Cambodian dictator Pol Pot. He regrets that the international community did not do more to stop the genocide in Cambodia while it was happening, and he calls for Pol Pot's remaining lieutenants to be brought to justice.

One of this century's most brutal and repressive dictators [has] died. Pol Pot, founder and leader of the Khmer Rouge, architect of the grisly genocide which claimed at least one million Cambodians between 1975 and 1979, died at the age of 73. While some may see Pol Pot's death as final closure on one of the most shockingly brutal and despotic reigns in history, his death should not absolve the international community from seeking full justice for the people of Cambodia.

The scars from Pol Pot's four-year reign of terror remain in Cambodia, and on the face of humanity. History will ask about us, Did they do enough? Did they do what they could? Did they really care? If those assessments were written today, the community of nations of this would be found wanting.

When Pol Pot and his Khmer Rouge captured the Cambodian capitol of Phnom Penh in April 1975, he and his lieutenants began a barbaric campaign to exterminate intellectuals, foreigners, bureaucrats, merchants, and countless others who did not fit Pol Pot's vision of a "pure" Cambodia. Thousands more were forced into slave labor camps, many eventually dying from starvation, torture, and disease.

Four years later in 1979, when Pol Pot and the Khmer Rouge were forced from power, left behind was a ghastly swath of death and carnage that counted at least one million Cambodians dead and a country still trying to cope with the ghosts of that era. Virtually every Cambodian knows or is related to someone whose life was extinguished.

Though Pol Pot was the [mastermind] of the killing fields of Cambodia, those in his inner circle were responsible for carrying out his commands. Many of Pol Pot's chief lieutenants still roam the Cambodian countryside, reportedly along the Thai border. Men like Khieu Samphan, former president of Kampuchea, Nuon Chea, former second in command and someone described as Pol Pot's "alter ego," and Ta Mok, a Khmer Rouge leader whose portfolio included killing Cambodians who had worked for the old Lon Nol government. Ta Mok was nicknamed "the Butcher."

The wanton killing did not end decades ago. In 1996 British mine clearer Christopher Howes and his interpreter, Houn Hourth, were abducted by Khmer Rouge henchmen and later led to a field and shot in the back. According to recent reports of interviews with Khmer Rouge officials, aides close to Pol Pot ordered the killing. Mr. Howes posed no threat to Pol Pot or the Khmer Rouge. Howes was in Cambodia working to make the country's fields safer for the Cambodian people by helping remove one-by-one the millions of landmines sown in the fields. . . .

We must not let Pol Pot's death diminish our resolve to apprehend and bring to justice those members of Pol Pot's inner circle who are equally guilty of crimes against humanity. History will judge us harshly if we fail in this critical task.

Patrick Leahy, "Seeking Justice in Cambodia," statement to the Senate Foreign Operations Appropriations Subcommittee, April 22, 1998.

Document 9: Bin Laden Justifies 9/11 Attacks and Vows There Will Be More Violence

In his first statement after the September 11, 2001, attacks, broadcast by the Arab television network Al Jazeera, Osama bin Laden claims that the United States is receiving retribution for the crimes it has committed around the world. He vows that the United States and its inhabitants will have no peace until there is peace in Palestine and the Western armed forces leave Saudi Arabia.

God Almighty hit the United States at its most vulnerable spot. He destroyed its greatest buildings.

Praise be to God.

Here is the United States. It was filled with terror from its north to its south and from its east to its west.

Praise be to God.

What the United States tastes today is a very small thing compared to what we have tasted for tens of years. . . .

May God mete them the punishment they deserve.

I say that the matter is clear and explicit.

In the aftermath of this event and now that senior US officials have spoken, beginning with Bush, the head of the world's infidels, and whoever supports him, every Muslim should rush to defend his religion. . . .

As for the United States, I tell it and its people these few words: I swear by Almighty God who raised the heavens without pillars that neither the United States nor he who lives in the United States will enjoy security before we can see it as a reality in Palestine and before all the infidel armies leave the land of Mohammed, may God's peace and blessing be upon him.

Osama bin Laden, audiotape, broadcast on Al Jazeera, October 2001.

Document 10: Bin Laden Reacts to the News of the 9/11 Attacks

In mid-November 2001, Osama bin Laden was under attack by U.S. and coalition forces in Afghanistan. Hiding out in a cave in the mountains of that country, he videotaped himself being interviewed by an unidentified "Shayk." In the interview, he describes the motivation of the September 11 attackers and the effect the attacks have had in rallying support to the cause of radical Islam.

UBL:[1] *(. . . Inaudible . . .)* when people see a strong horse and a weak horse, by nature, they will like the strong horse. This is only one goal; those who want people to worship the lord of the people, without following that doctrine, will be following the doctrine of Muhammad, peace be upon him.

(UBL quotes several short and incomplete Hadith [Islamic scripture] verses, as follows):

"I was ordered to fight the people until they say there is no god but Allah, and his prophet Muhammad.". . .

UBL: *(. . . Inaudible . . .)* we calculated in advance the number of casualties from the enemy, who would be killed based on the position of the tower. We calculated that the floors that would be hit would be three or four floors. I was the most optimistic of them all. *(. . . Inaudible . . .)* due to my experience in this field, I was thinking that the fire from the gas in the plane would melt the iron structure of the building and collapse the area where the plane hit and all the floors above it only. This is all that we had hoped for.

Shaykh: Allah be praised.

UBL: We were at *(. . . inaudible . . .)* when the event took place. We had notification since the previous Thursday that the event would take place that day. We had finished our work that day and had the radio on. It was 5:30 P.M. our time. I was sitting with Dr. Ahmad Abu-al-(Khair). Immediately, we heard the news that a plane had hit the World Trade Center. We turned the radio station to the news from Washington. The news continued and no mention of the attack until the end. At the end of the newscast, they reported that a plane just hit the World Trade Center.

Shaykh: Allah be praised.

UBL: After a little while, they announced that another plane had hit the World Trade Center. The brothers who heard the news were overjoyed by it. . . .

Shaykh: "Fight them, Allah will torture them, with your hands, he will torture them. He will deceive them and he will give you victory. Allah will forgive the believers, he is knowledgeable about everything."

1. UBL stands for Usama bin Laden. Usama is an alternate spelling of Osama.

Shaykh: No doubt it is a clear victory. Allah has bestowed on us . . . honor on us . . . and he will give us blessing and more victory during this holy month of Ramadan. And this is what everyone is hoping for. Thank Allah America came out of its caves. We hit her the first hit and the next one will hit her with the hands of the believers, the good believers, the strong believers.

Osama bin Laden, videotaped interview, broadcast on Al Jazeera, November 2001.

For Further Research

Books

Gerry Adams, *Before the Dawn: An Autobiography*. New York: William Morrow, 1996.

Yonah Alexander and Michael S. Swetnam, *Usama bin Laden's al-Qaida: Profile of a Terrorist Network*. Ardsley, NY: Transnational, 2001.

Tai Sung An, *Mao Tse-tung's Cultural Revolution*. Farmington Hills, MI: Pegasus, 1972.

Stefan Aust, *The Baader-Meinhof Group: The Inside Story of a Phenomenon*. Trans. Anthea Bell. London: Bodley Head, 1987.

Christopher Dobson and Ronald Payne, *War Without End: The Terrorists: An Intelligence Dossier*. London: Harrap, 1986.

John Follain, *Jackal: The Complete Story of the Legendary Terrorist, Carlos the Jackal*. New York: Arcade, 1998.

Gustavo Gorriti-Ellenbogen, *The Shining Path: A History of the Millenarian War in Peru*. Trans. Robin Kirk. Chapel Hill: University of North Carolina Press, 1999.

Mark S. Hamm, *In Bad Company: America's Terrorist Underground*. Boston: Northeastern University Press, 2002.

Michael L. Kennedy, *The Jacobin Clubs in the French Revolution, 1793–1795*. New York: Oxford University Press, 2000.

Ben Kiernan, *The Pol Pot Regime: Race, Power, and Genocide in*

Cambodia Under the Khmer Rouge, 1975–1979. New Haven, CT: Yale University Press, 1996.

Feigon Lee, *Mao: A Reinterpretation.* Chicago: Ivan R. Dee, 2002.

Daniel Levitas, *The Terrorist Next Door: The Militia Movement and the Radical Right.* New York: Thomas Dunne Books/St. Martin's, 2002.

Michael Mello, *The United States of America Versus Theodore John Kaczynski: Ethics, Power, and the Invention of the Unabomber.* New York: Context, 1999.

Lou Michel, *American Terrorist: Timothy McVeigh and the Oklahoma City Bombing.* New York: Regan, 2001.

Daniel Myerson, *Blood and Splendor: The Lives of Five Tyrants, from Nero to Saddam Hussein.* New York: Perennial, 2000.

Riccardo Orizio, *Talk of the Devil: Encounters with Seven Dictators.* Trans. Avril Bardoni. New York: Walker, 2003.

Barry M. Rubin, *Yasir Arafat: A Political Biography.* New York: Oxford University Press, 2003.

Eli Sagan, *Citizens and Cannibals: The French Revolution, the Struggle for Modernity, and the Origins of Ideological Terror.* Lanham, MD: Rowman & Littlefield, 2001.

Jack Sargeant, ed., *Guns, Death, Terror: 1960's and 1970's Revolutionaries, Urban Guerrillas, and Terrorists.* London: Creation, 2003.

Sasson Sofer, *Begin: An Anatomy of Leadership.* New York: B. Blackwell, 1988.

Robert W. Thurston, *Life and Terror in Stalin's Russia, 1934–1941.* New Haven, CT: Yale University Press, 1996.

Periodicals

Robert C. Baker, "When Baader Met Meinhof," *Village Voice,* June 11, 2003.

Miguel Esperanza, "Terrorism in Peru," *America*, June 20, 1992.

Barbara J. Fraser, "Report Says 70,000 Dead or Disappeared in Peru," *National Catholic Reporter*, September 19, 2003.

Nicole Gaouette, "Trial of Jackal Aids Antiterrorist Cause," *Christian Science Monitor*, December 15, 1997.

Michael O. Garvey, "Death in Terre Haute: The Execution of Timothy McVeigh," *Commonweal*, July 13, 2001.

Jonathon Gatehouse, "Misunderstood Warriors or Terror's Prodigal Sons?" *Maclean's*, December 15, 2003.

Stephen Goode and Eli Lehrer, "The Evil Twins: Josef Stalin and Mao Tse-tung," *Insight on the News*, March 22, 1999.

History Today, "The Dictators, the Second World War, and the Holocaust," November 2003.

Mansoor Ijaz, "Saddam and the Terrorists," *National Review*, June 30, 2003.

Henry K. Miller, "Fatal Attraction: Che Guevara, Carlos the Jackal, Andreas Baader: These Are the Faces of Radical Terrorist Chic," *New Statesman*, October 28, 2002.

Tom Morganthau and Mark Hosenball, "Probing the Mind of a Killer," *Newsweek*, April 15, 1996.

Dennis A. Pluchinsky, "Germany's Red Army Faction: An Obituary," *Studies in Conflict & Terrorism*, April–June 1993.

Dennis B. Ross, "Yasir Arafat: Think Again," *Foreign Policy*, July/August 2002.

Ian D. Thatcher, "Nazism and Stalinism," *History Review*, March 2003.

George Wehrfritz, "Mao Was the Best Emperor of All Time," *Newsweek*, May 6, 1996.

Internet Sources

BBC News Online Service: Who Is Osama Bin Laden?, http://news.bbc.co.uk/hi/english/world/south_asia/newsid_155000/155236.stm. The British Broadcasting Service's profile of Bin Laden. The page has links to more sites about Bin Laden, as well as streaming video of a BBC "Panorama" program on the terrorist.

Modern History Sourcebook: Stalin's Purges, 1935, www.fordham.edu/halsall/mod/1936purges.html. The Modern History Sourcebook project compiles original documents in translated into English. This page contains a translation of Soviet textbooks, showing how the terror of Stalin's purges was explained to Soviet students.

Naval Postgraduate School: Profiles of Terrorist Groups, http://library.nps.navy.mil/home/tgp/tgpndx.htm. Very useful for site for those in search of basic knowledge about various terrorist groups. Each group designated as a terrorist organization by the U.S. government has an entry; most entries include a link to a brief dossierlike description of the group's history and leaders.

Office of the Coordinator for Counterterrorism of the U.S. Department of State: Patterns of Global Terrorism 2002, www.state.gov/s/ct/rls/pgtrpt/2002. The State Department is required by Congress to present an annual report on terrorism worldwide. This site has links to the report in both html and downloadable pdf format, as well as archives of past reports.

PBS Frontline: Hunting Bin Laden: Investigating Osama Bin Laden, His Supporters, and the U.S. Campaign Against Them, www.pbs.org/wgbh/pages/frontline/shows/binladen. Based on the Public Broadcasting Service's *Frontline* episode on Bin Laden, this site has biographical information on Bin Laden, a link to a video interview with the terrorist, and additional links with information on other al Qaeda terrorists.

Salon: The Patriot, by Gary Kamiya, http://dir.salon.com/
books/2001/04/07/mcveigh/index.html?sid=1023243. An
in-depth profile of Timothy McVeigh, accompanied by
an online discussion forum.

Web Site

Terrorism Research Center, www.terrorism.com. The Terrorism Research Center is a fee-based subscription site
that features various documents and research reports
about terrorist attacks, groups, and leaders. The site offers a substantial amount of free content, although subscription is required for access to many of the reports
and documents.

Index

Abu Iyad, 139, 140, 142–43
Afghanistan
  Soviet invasion of, 14,
    25–26
  following Soviet
    withdrawal, 35–36
  as a training ground for
    Islamic mujahideen, 32
  U.S. war with, 56–60
  see also Taliban, the
Alfred P. Murrah Building
  bombing (1995), 188,
  195–97
Algeria
  armed revolt desired by
    citizens in, 128–29
  independence movement
    in, 126
    Arafat inspired by,
      142–43
    neutralizing enemies of,
      129–30
    police response to,
      132–33
    raids by, 130–32
    secret organization of,
      127–28
    violent acts by, 130
  rejection of elections in,
    127
Annan, Kofi, 61

Ansar, Masadat Al-, 27
Anti-Semitism, in Eastern
  Europe, 90
Arafat, Yasir, 19
  arrest of, in Egypt, 140
  birth of, 136
  construction business of,
    141–42
  founding of Fatah and,
    139–40, 142
  influences on, 142–43
  name of, 136–38
  university days of, 141
  warfare studied by, 139,
    140
Arnett, Peter, 46
Azerbaijan, 48
Azzam, AbdAllah Yussuf,
  26, 27, 42–43

Baader-Meinhof gang, 20,
  158, 166
Barère, Bertrand, 70
Begin, Menachem, 19, 117
Ben Bella, Ahmed, 18–19
  arrest of, 132–33
  resistance organized by,
    127–28
Bergen, Peter L., 45
Billaud-Varenne, Jean
  Nicolas, 71